BRITISH FILMS 1944-1973

ANOTHER WORLD

by

Andy Coleby

Grosvenor House
Publishing Limited

This book is published by
Grosvenor House Publishing Ltd
28-30 High Street, Guildford, Surrey, GU1 3EL.
www. grosvenorhousepublishing. co. uk

A CIP record for this book
is available from the British Library

ISBN 978-1-78148-658-0

DEDICATION

To my late grandmother, Margaret Coleby (1894–1984)

For looking after me and taking my brother and I to the Uxbridge Odeon and Uxbridge Regal on many occasions in the 1960's. She knew the actor Finlay Currie (1878–1968) and often had a Guinness and a cheese roll with him. He had success in scores of British and Hollywood roles, including Magwitch in "Great Expectations" (covered in this book). A notable part that he played was one of the three wise men in the 1959 film "Ben Hur". I can therefore say that my grandmother knew one of the three wise men.

INTRODUCTION

This is a very welcome addition to the lexicon of film history. A lot of the films selected may be unknown to you and probably would not find their way into the majority of filmographies which makes it all the more worthy and interesting to the genuine film connoisseur and this is not because Andy included one of our films – but it helped.

Ray Galton & Alan Simpson

FOREWORD

There is a famous and perhaps over-used quote from the introduction to L.P. Hartley's 1953 novel "The Go-Between" - "The past is a foreign country, they do things differently there".

This book is about people doing things differently over four decades. I have had deep affection for British films made during 1944–1973, ever since I was a child. Many happy hours were spent watching old British movies on our dodgy Radio Rentals' black and white "Baird" brand television set and later on an amazingly reliable Hitachi colour one.

Time and time again I loved seeing the likes of "North West Frontier", "Hell Drivers" and "The Titfield Thunderbolt". I closely watched the beguiling stars and wonderful character players and felt as if I knew Kenneth More, Stanley Baker and John Gregson.

I have always wanted to go back in time, rather than having the usual predilection for going forward, but not too far back, perhaps 1960. Alas, this is not possible and even if it was, I would feel paranoid about getting stuck there! However, I can have a tiny glimpse of 1960, as if through a keyhole and "Doctor in Love", with its rich period air can transport me back quite easily.

I have seen and written reviews of about 1,500 British films from this period, alas to publish all of them in book form would entail several volumes. Because of this I have selected just 100 of my absolute favourites. Most of these I have seen between five and ten times each and I have found them unbreakable, they are still very entertaining after all these viewings. Many were critically derided on release and are still dismissed. Others will no doubt only be familiar to people born long before our fast changing technological age. No doubt some people reading my selection, especially "cineastes" (how I hate that pretentious word) and "film buffs" (two words which suggest you are a dithering bore), will recoil in horror at my choices.

The fact that I seemed to like strange films and disliked so many "classics" spurred me on to write this book. There is a lot of snobbery in movie criticism. Movies are placed on a pedestal or buried. I have never been a fan of "The Third Man" or "Kind Hearts and Coronets" or "Lawrence of Arabia", if you are you will be shocked by this book.

I was always fascinated by the films that were overlooked, forgotten or neglected. I love "Inn For Trouble", "Light Up The Sky" and "The Bargee". This is their story and the story of 97 other films.

I believe the function of a critic is to stimulate opinions, not to try to agree with what a "typical person" might like, as there is no such thing as a "typical person". I do not expect that most of my choices will be popular with "film buffs", but you have to agree I have some nerve choosing many of them!

Andy Coleby

"That's part of your problem you know, you haven't seen enough movies. All of life's riddles are answered in the movies" Steve Martin as "Davis" in "Grand Canyon" (Lawrence Kasdan, Meg Kasdan, Twentieth Century Fox 1991)

MY 100 FAVOURITE FILMS

For a selection of other one star films please see the back of this book.

RATINGS AND ABOUT THIS BOOK

RATINGS:

*****	A real gem
****	Solid entertainment
***	Well above average
**	Above average
*	Generally agreeable, but flawed

Why 1944–1973?

The British cinema started to really enter the modern age in 1944, but by 1973 was losing its' innocence.

It should be pointed out that these entries are personal choices and do not take account of prevailing ideas as to what is regarded as a good or classic film in this period.

A note on circuit and approximate release date:

The date could vary as some cinemas outside major towns and cities had to wait longer to receive a release. Also, the supporting feature could change if shown by a cinema not on the regular three (later two) circuits.

News:	From January 1944 – December 1973
Pop Hits:	From January 1953 – December 1973
Popular TV:	From October 1955 – December 1973
Popular New Cars:	From January 1944 – December 1973

ALBERT R.N. (1953)

RATING: **

SYNOPSIS: In 1944 the latest arrival at a prisoner of war camp for naval officers in Germany is a US Navy Air Force Lieutenant. The latest escape goes wrong and restrictions are imposed on the prisoners. However, one of the inmates proposes getting a prisoner out by replacing him with a life like dummy: "Albert" who will take his place at roll calls.

REVIEW: A near forgotten POW camp film and one of the best, it's modest, likeable and easy to take. Scripted by Vernon Harris and Guy Morgan, it was based on a stage play by Edward R Sammis and Guy Morgan. They have placed well rounded characters into believable and sometimes touching situations. Lewis Gilbert directs carefully and helps to make this thoughtful and absorbing. Understated playing from Anthony Steel and Jack Warner (both "By permission of the J Arthur Rank Organisation") and the rest of the cast helps. Neat, unpretentious and better than "The Colditz Story", made two years later.

CAST: Anthony Steel; Jack Warner; Robert Beatty; William Sylvester; Anton Diffring; Eddie Byrne; Guy Middleton; Paul Carpenter; Michael Balfour; Moultrie Kelsall; Frederick Valk; Peter Jones; Geoffrey Hibbert; Frederick Schiller; Walter Gotell; Peter Swanwick.

PRODUCTION COMPANY–ORIGINAL UK DISTRIBUTOR:

Daniel M Angel/Dial Films (uncredited) – Eros Films

NOT AVAILABLE ON DVD

FILM STUDIO: Nettlefold Studios Ltd., Walton on Thames

LOCATIONS: The camp was built in countryside near Dorking, Surrey

CIRCUIT AND APPROXIMATE RELEASE DATE:

Gaumont - December 1953 - Cert U - Supported by "Love In Pawn" (GB "B" film)

RUNNING TIME ON TV: 79 minutes

FORMAT: Black and White

IN THE UK AROUND THE TIME OF RELEASE

NEWS: Commercial television will appear in 1955, around this time the House of Lords voted in favour of the proposal.

POP HITS: Answer Me - Frankie Laine; Answer Me - David Whitfield

POPULAR NEW CARS: Austin A30 (1951–1956); Standard 8 (1953–1959)

ARABESQUE (1966)

RATING: *

SYNOPSIS: A man posing as an optician kills a patient and takes out a message hidden in his glasses. The killer is private secretary to a Middle East shipping millionaire. An Oxford university professor, an expert in Egyptian hieroglyphics, meets the Prime Minister of a Middle East state who is the subject of a plot against him. Visiting the shipping tycoon, his mistress then warns the professor of the danger he's in and both go on the run.

REVIEW: A lightweight spy film mixing thrills and comedy, made palatable by flashy handling. Director Stanley Donen dresses it up with lots of strange camera angles, perhaps to try to disguise the paucity of substance. Many great location sequences help, as does Henry Mancini's typically first rate score. Maurice Binder provides one of those wonderful opening titles sequences which only existed in the 1960's, having already had much experience designing the James Bond ones. The script by Julian Mitchell, Stanley Price and Pierre Marton, based on Gordon Cotler's novel "The Cypher" is basically a cartoon strip, really and is highly episodic. Leads Gregory Peck and Sophia Loren look good, but struggle with the trivial goings on. Very much of its time which is a big part of its appeal.

CAST: Gregory Peck; Sophia Loren; Alan Badel; Kieron Moore; Carl Duering; John Merivale; Duncan Lamont; George Coulouris; Ernest Clark; Harry Locke; Harold Kasket.

PRODUCTION COMPANY–ORIGINAL UK DISTRIBUTOR:

Stanley Donen Enterprises Ltd/Universal – Rank Film Distributors

AVAILABLE ON DVD

FILM STUDIO: Pinewood

LOCATIONS: Ascot Racecourse and Hurley, Berkshire; London including Trafalgar Square and Heathrow Airport; Wales; Oxford.

CIRCUIT AND APPROXIMATE RELEASE DATE:

Odeon – September 1966 – Cert A - Supported by "Love and Kisses"

RUNNING TIME ON TV: 101 minutes

FORMAT: Technicolor - Techniscope

IN THE UK AROUND THE TIME OF RELEASE

NEWS: Ronald "Buster" Edwards is arrested in connection with the Great Train Robbery of 1963.

POP HITS: Yellow Submarine and Eleanor Rigby - The Beatles; All Or Nothing - The Small Faces

POPULAR TV: Coronation Street (ITV); Till Death Us Do Part (sitcom, BBC)

POPULAR NEW CARS: Austin 1800 (1964–1975) - Ford Cortina (Mk 1) (1962–1966)

THE ASPHYX (1973)

RATING: **

SYNOPSIS: In 1875, whilst working on psychic research, an aristocrat discovers "smudges" appearing on photographs of people who are about to die. He believes that these marks show the human soul at the moment it departs from the body. After experimenting with a guinea pig, he manages to contain the spirit of death or "asphyx" and prevent the animal's demise. Will the experiment work on him?

REVIEW: A genuinely different and quite compelling blend of science fiction and horror, much better than Hammer explo-pics. The script by Brian Comport unfolds in an admirably straight way and is neatly constructed and intelligent. There's also excellent playing from lead Robert Stephens, he's never been better on screen than here. Peter Newbrook directs in a tight and careful way and is given admirable assistance by John Stoll's claustrophobic production design. The title figure is one of the most chilling creatures ever seen in any movie. Contains nice main theme music by Bill McGuffie.

CAST: Robert Stephens; Robert Powell; Jane Lapotaire; Alex Scott; Ralph Arliss; Fiona Walker; Tony Caunter; Terry Scully; John Lawrence; David Grey; Paul Bacon.

PRODUCTION COMPANY–ORIGINAL UK DISTRIBUTOR:

Glendale - Scotia-Barber

AVAILABLE ON DVD: US import only (Region 1)

FILM STUDIO: Shepperton

CIRCUIT AND APPROXIMATE RELEASE DATE:

Odeon - March 1973 - Cert AA - Supported by choice of two re–released "A" films

RUNNING TIME ON TV: 83 minutes

FORMAT: Eastmancolor - Todd-AO

IN THE UK AROUND THE TIME OF RELEASE

NEWS: The new London Bridge was opened by the Queen.

POP HITS: Cum On Feel The Noize - Slade; The Twelfth Of Never – Donny Osmond

POPULAR TV: This Is Your Life (ITV); The Dick Emery Show (comedy series, BBC)

POPULAR NEW CARS: Morris Marina (1971–1980); Hillman Hunter (1966–1979)

THE BARGEE (1964)

RATING: ***

SYNOPSIS: A barge owner and his slow witted cousin arrive back from Birmingham on a dual barge. They go to a British Waterways Settlement office and agree to transport fifty tons of lemon peel in barrels. During their journey from Brentford to Boxmoor in Hertfordshire, the bargee, a casanova, plans to visit several of his girlfriends who live along the route. Romantic problems ensue.

REVIEW: This is worth seeing just for the extensive canal side sequences, all are highly engaging. Along with the rest of the film they're beautifully shot by Harry Waxman in Technicolor. Ray Galton and Alan Simpson's clever script is full of amusing and likeable characters and has dozens of very funny scenes and lines. There's also a lot of perception here and it's breezy and upbeat. As for the chauvinism, the lead played by an excellent Harry H Corbett is an angel compared to "Alfie". Duncan Wood directs with confidence and real flair, it's sad that he concentrated on television and didn't make lots more movies. In support Ronnie Barker and Derek Nimmo are seen in great form, but Eric Sykes is over the top and unfunny. The period air, partly due to the detailed art direction of Robert Jones is a big part of its appeal, as is Frank Cordell's lovely score. Admittedly some scenes are a bit self-conscious, but this is stylish, different and observant and one of the most under-rated British film comedies produced in the 1960's.

CAST: Harry H Corbett; Hugh Griffith; Julia Foster; Eric Sykes; Ronnie Barker; Eric Barker; Derek Nimmo; Miriam Karlin; Norman Bird; Richard Briers; Brian Wilde; George A Cooper; Jo Rowbotham; Grazina Frame; Edwin Apps; Godfrey Winn (voice only - on radio at start). UNBILLED CAST: Patricia Hayes; Michael Robbins; Ed Devereux; Rita Webb; Wally Patch; Ronnie Brody; Eileen Way; Sidney Vivian.

PRODUCTION COMPANY–ORIGINAL UK DISTRIBUTOR:

Associated British Picture Corporation/Galton Simpson - Warner-Pathe

AVAILABLE ON DVD

FILM STUDIO: The Elstree Studios of Associated British Picture Corporation

LOCATIONS: Marworth Top Lock, Bulbourne, Hertfordshire; Brentford Lock, London Borough of Hounslow; Hanwell Locks, London Borough of Ealing

CIRCUIT AND APPROXIMATE RELEASE DATE:

ABC - May 1964 - Cert A – In the top ten box office hits of the year

RUNNING TIME ON TV: 101 minutes

FORMAT: Technicolor -Techniscope

NOTE: Corbett was then a big star on TV in the BBC series "Steptoe and Son", written by Ray Galton and Alan Simpson, who were to achieve legendary status.

IN THE UK AROUND THE TIME OF RELEASE

NEWS: The War Office becomes the Ministry of Defence;the Great Train robbers are sentenced.

POP HITS: Don't Throw Your Love Away - The Searchers; A World Without Love – Peter and Gordon

POPULAR TV: Coronation Street (ITV); No Hiding Place (crime drama series, ITV)

POPULAR NEW CARS: Ford Zodiac (Mk III) (1962–1966); MGB Roadster (Mk I) (1962–1967)

BARNACLE BILL (1957)

RATING: **

SYNOPSIS: After receiving a medal from Lloyds of London, a middle aged naval captain tells a local newspaper reporter his family history in the navy. He also recalls his inability to go to sea due to chronic seasickness. As a result he buys a pier in a seaside resort, telling the staff that he will run it like a ship. Problems with the police and council officials follow.

REVIEW: The penultimate Ealing comedy (Davy was the last released), but made at Borehamwood for MGM, is pleasingly eccentric. It has a modest and lightweight feel, but is easy to take and very likeable. The script by T.E.B Clarke is scrappily constructed, but always good natured and nicely and unusually anti-establishment. Charles Frend directs with tongue in cheek and gets a wry performance from Alec Guinness - he underplays splendidly. In support there are lots of seasoned character players to boost it further. Douglas Slocombe's radiant photography and John Addison's jaunty score are additional pleasures. Agreeable location sequences add to the fun.

CAST: Alec Guinness; Irene Browne; Maurice Denham; Percy Herbert; Victor Maddern; Allan Cuthbertson; Lionel Jeffries; Harold Goodwin; George Rose; Richard Wattis; Donald Pleasence; Warren Mitchell; (voice dubbed by another actor); Lloyd Lamble; Harry Locke; Frederick Piper; Miles Malleson; William Mervyn; Joan Hickson; Sam Kydd; Toke Townley; Charles Lloyd Pack; John Horsley; Elsie Wagstaffe; Anthony Sagar; Newton Blick; Fred Griffiths; Donald Churchill; Max Butterfield; Eric Pohlmann; Jackie Collins (yes THE Jackie Collins); Derek Waring; Mike Morgan. Also others.

PRODUCTION COMPANY–ORIGINAL UK DISTRIBUTOR:

MGM/Ealing Films - MGM

AVAILABLE ON DVD

FILM STUDIO: M.G.M. British Studios (Borehamwood)

LOCATIONS: Hunstanton Pier, Norfolk

CIRCUIT AND APPROXIMATE RELEASE DATE:

ABC – January 1958 – Cert U

RUNNING TIME ON TV: 83 minutes

FORMAT: Black and White

IN THE UK AROUND THE TIME OF RELEASE

NEWS: Sir Edmund Hillary, who conquered Everest in 1953, arrives at the South Pole, the first overland explorer to do so since Scott in 1912.

POP HITS: Jailhouse Rock - Elvis Presley; Great Balls Of Fire - Little Richard

POPULAR TV: Take Your Pick (quiz series, ITV); The Army Game (sitcom, ITV)

POPULAR NEW CARS: Morris Cowley (1954–1959); Standard Eight (1953–1959)

BEDAZZLED (1967)

RATING: ****

SYNOPSIS: For six years, a short order cook in a Wimpy Bar has, unbeknown to her, secretly been in love with a waitress he works with. After failing to hang himself over his despair at seeing her with a boyfriend, he is approached by the devil, who poses as a nightclub owner. The cook agrees to let him have his soul in exchange for seven wishes.

REVIEW: This is easily the best film made by the fantastic comedy duo Peter Cook and Dudley Moore who had enjoyed considerable television success previously. Both are in absolute top form and are a joy to watch at every turn. Cook also wrote the script from a story by Moore and it's hilarious and delightfully cynical, but never sour, a real achievement. It's full of acidic outbursts and offbeat gags and totally different to other movie comedies. Legendary Hollywood musical director Stanley Donen ("Singin' In The Rain") handles it with freewheeling assurance and awesome professionalism. One of the most classy and clever film comedies of the 1960's. Glowingly photographed in De Luxe colour by Austin Dempster and there's a nice score by Dudley Moore too.

CAST: Peter Cook; Dudley Moore; Eleanor Bron; Raquel Welch; Michael Bates; Barry Humphries; Michael Trubshawe; Charles Lloyd Pack; Robert Russell; Lockwood West; Robin Hawdon; Bernard Spear; Alba; Howard Goorney; Parnell McGarry; Danielle Noel; Evelyn More; Betty Cooper. UNBILLED CAST: Erik Chitty.

PRODUCTION COMPANY–ORIGINAL UK DISTRIBUTOR:

Stanley Donen Enterprises Limited - Twentieth Century Fox

AVAILABLE ON DVD

FILM STUDIO: St. Johns Wood Studios, London

LOCATIONS: High Street, Borehamwood (The Wimpy); Piccadilly Circus; The Post Office Tower; Syon Park.

CIRCUIT AND APPROXIMATE RELEASE DATE:

Odeon - April 1968 – Cert A – Supported by "Track Of Thunder"

RUNNING TIME ON TV: 99 minutes

FORMAT: De Luxe colour -Techniscope

IN THE UK AROUND THE TIME OF RELEASE

NEWS: Legendary formula one driver Jim Clark, 32, racing for Lotus dies after crashing at 170 miles an hour in Hockenheimring, Germany; Enoch Powell gives his notorious "Rivers of Blood" speech at Birmingham. Conservative party leader Edward Heath sacks him the next day.

POP HITS: Congratulations - Cliff Richard; What A Wonderful World and Cabaret - Louis Armstrong

POPULAR TV: Coronation Street (ITV); Eurovision Song Contest (BBC)

POPULAR NEW CARS: Morris 1100 (1962–1974); Hillman Imp (1963–1976)

THE BELLES OF ST.TRINIAN'S (1954)

RATING: **

SYNOPSIS: A rich Arab decides to send his young daughter to the notoriously unconventional "St Trinian's" girls' boarding school. The headmaster's bookmaker brother then persuades him to take back his expelled daughter so that she can find out about the Arab's horse which is stabled nearby. In the meantime, a woman police constable poses as a games mistress at the school to investigate crimes committed by the pupils.

REVIEW: This is worth seeing for its wonderful cast alone, notably George Cole. He's hilarious as Flash Harry the spiv, one of the greatest characters of British cinema. Also seen in top form are Alastair Sim (in a dual role), Joyce Grenfell, Lloyd Lamble and Richard Wattis. As a whole the film is a bit too lumpy and episodic, but it's also splendidly cosy as well as being delightfully anarchic. The script by Frank Launder, Sidney Gilliat and Val Valentine was inspired by "the original drawings of the girls and staff by Ronald Searle". They cram this full of marvellous characters and lots of very funny scenes. Frank Launder also provided the breezy, highly assured and tongue in cheek direction. He's ably assisted by Stanley Pavey's well lit photography and Malcolm Arnold's typically accomplished score. Not the least of its virtues is the period atmosphere and Joseph Bato's art direction is an integral part of this. Often rough and ready, but frequently endearing too.

CAST: Alastair Sim; Joyce Grenfell; George Cole; Lloyd Lamble; Richard Wattis; Sid James; Beryl Reid.; Hermione Baddeley; Irene Handl; Guy Middleton; Joan Sims; Renee Houston; Eric Pohlmann; Belinda Lee; Michael Ripper; Mary Merrall; Arthur Howard;

Andree Melly; Betty Ann Davies; Jerry Verno; Vivienne Wood; Tommy Duggan. Windsor Cottage (the horse). Also others. UNBILLED CAST: Barbara Windsor; Shirley Eaton; Dilys Laye; Michael Balfour; Roger Delgado; Ronald Searle; Damaris Hayman; Catherine Feller; Myrette Morven; Stuart Saunders; Henry Longhurst; Ann Way. And many others.

PRODUCTION COMPANY–ORIGINAL UK DISTRIBUTOR:

Sidney Gilliat-Frank Launder/London Films - British Lion

AVAILABLE ON DVD

FILM STUDIO: Shepperton

LOCATIONS: All Nations College, Easneye, Stanstead Abbots, Hertfordshire

CIRCUIT AND APPROXIMATE RELEASE DATE:

Gaumont – October 1954 - Cert U – Supported by "The End Of The Road" (GB "B" film) In the top ten box office hits of the year.

RUNNING TIME ON TV: 87 minutes

FORMAT: Black and White

IN THE UK AROUND THE TIME OF RELEASE

NEWS: Roger Bannister runs one mile in just less than four minutes.

POP HITS: Three Coins in The Fountain - Frank Sinatra; Hold My Hand – Don Cornell

POPULAR NEW CARS: Austin A40 Cambridge (1954–1958); Vauxhall Cresta (E) (1954–1957)

THE BELSTONE FOX (1973)

RATING: **

SYNOPSIS: Late one night, a huntsman who is in charge of his hunt's foxhounds, is visited by an old friend. He's brought along a tiny fox cub whose mother has been killed deliberately by two men. Taking his wife's advice he lets one of his foxhounds feed and look after it. As it grows up it becomes inseparable from another of the hounds. However the friendship causes problems when the hunt begins.

REVIEW: A warm and touching drama, all the more appealing as it's a rare example of a British film with a rural setting. It's worth seeing for its Somerset locations (see below) whose splendour is captured by the superb Eastmancolor photography of John Wilcox and James Allen. Based on a novel, "The Ballad of The Belstone Fox", by David Rook, the script was written by James Hill. It's a bit scrappy, but is pleasingly different and has believable characters. The under - rated Eric Porter is in great form here and out-acts everyone easily. Hill also directed and shows a real feel for the countryside, handling the virtually continuous countryside locations expertly. Oddly uncommercial, wherein much of is charm lies. Laurie Johnson's typically good score has a beautiful main theme. An overlooked and sadly under-rated film.

CAST: Eric Porter; Jeremy Kemp; Bill Travers; Rachel Roberts; Dennis Waterman; Heather Wright. UNBILLED CAST: Ralph Arliss.

PRODUCTIONCOMPANY–ORIGINAL UK DISTRIBUTOR:

The Rank Organisation/Independent Artists – Rank Film Distributors

AVAILABLE ON DVD

FILM STUDIO: Pinewood

LOCATIONS: Merridge, North Petherton and others in Somerset.

CIRCUIT AND APPROXIMATE RELEASE DATE:

Odeon - January 1974 – Cert A – Supported by a choice of two re-released films including The Plank (GB short film)

RUNNING TIME ON TV: 99 minutes

FORMAT: Eastmancolor; Todd - AO 35

NOTE: Top billed Eric Porter became very famous six years before as Soames in the BBC's hit television series "The Forsyte Saga".

IN THE UK AROUND THE TIME OF RELEASE

NEWS: The three day week was introduced to conserve dwindling coal stocks during a miners' strike.

POP HITS: Merry Xmas Everybody - Slade; You Won't Find Another Fool Like Me - The New Seekers

POPULAR TV: This Is Your Life (ITV); The Val Doonican Show (variety show, BBC)

POPULAR NEW CARS: Austin Allegro (1973–1982); Ford Escort (Mk I) (1968–1975)

THE BLUE MAX (1966)

RATING: ****

SYNOPSIS: After fighting on the Western Front in France in 1916, as a soldier, a German Corporal becomes a pilot. He then determines to win the German flying medal "The Blue Max," and is relentless in his plan to shoot down the twenty enemy planes needed to secure it. However, his arrogant and unfeeling behaviour soon make him unpopular with his fellow pilots.

REVIEW: This has terrific impact in the first half, but is still quite compulsive the rest of the time. John Guillermin's assured and stylish direction rises above the lumpy storyline. The screenplay was written by David Pursall, Jack Seddon and Gerald Hanley and the book it was based on (by Jack D Hunter) was adapted by Ben Barzman and Basilio Franchina. There is intelligence in their work and it contains many powerful scenes. It's worth seeing just for the amazing flying sequences, these are superbly handled by Anthony Squire, the Aerial Unit Director. Quite breathtaking, they are as good as you are likely to see in any film. Also greatly impressing is the wonderful score by the reliable Jerry Goldsmith, who composed a particularly good main theme. As for the cast, George Peppard has never been better and lights up the screen here. He's well supported by James Mason, Jeremy Kemp and especially Karl Michael Vogler. Alas, Ursula Andress drags things down. A likeable, big scale war picture with much of its appeal coming from the fact that it's so different, as it's so cynical. The action scenes on the ground also deserve a mention, they're expertly staged too. Generally highly entertaining stuff.

CAST: George Peppard; Ursula Andress; James Mason; Jeremy Kemp; Karl Michael Vogler; Anton Diffring; Harry Towb; Derren Nesbitt; Derek Newark; Peter Woodthorpe; Loni Von Friedl; Frederich Ledebur; Alex Scott. Also others.

PRODUCTIONCOMPANY–ORIGINAL UK DISTRIBUTOR:

Twentieth Century Fox Productions - Twentieth Century Fox

AVAILABLE ON DVD

FILM STUDIO: Ardmore Studios, Bray, Ireland

LOCATIONS: Ireland: County Wicklow, County Dublin. County Cork, County Kildare

CIRCUIT AND APPROXIMATE RELEASE DATE:

Odeon - January 1967 – Cert A – In the top fourteen non roadshow box office hits of the year.

RUNNING TIME ON TV: 149 minutes

FORMAT: De Luxe colour – Cinemascope

IN THE UK AROUND THE TIME OF RELEASE

NEWS: England's victorious 1966 World Cup winning manager Alf Ramsey receives a Knighthood; The Forsyte Saga is broadcast on BBC2.

POP HITS: Green, Green Grass of Home - Tom Jones; Morningtown Ride -The Seekers

POPULAR TV: Take Your Pick (quiz series, ITV); The Morecambe And Wise Show (ITV)

POPULAR NEW CARS: Hillman Minx (1966–1977); Morris 1100 (1963–1974)

BLUE MURDER AT ST.TRINIAN'S (1957)

RATING: **

SYNOPSIS: "Flash" Harry Edwards, an "entrepreneur", meets a wealthy prince in his Rome villa and discusses his marriage bureau, agreeing to introduce some St.Trinian's schoolgirls. When Harry arrives back at the school he finds that the army has taken over due to the pupils' unruliness. Learning of a competition involving the Ministry of Education, he organises a break- in at their offices to make sure that the St Trinian's entry will have the correct answers. They subsequently win the trip to Rome, horrifying the officials. Soon after a male jewel thief travels to the school and is blackmailed into dressing up and replacing their headmistress for the journey to Rome.

REVIEW: The second and second best "St Trinian's" film. It isn't as solid and well rounded as the original, but has dozens of splendid gags. As in the previous entry, the cast is in superb form with George Cole, Joyce Grenfell, Lionel Jeffries and especially Terry-Thomas (who enters half way through) a delight. In support Thorley Walters, Lloyd Lamble and Richard Wattis, all excellent character players are great too. The script was by Frank Launder, Sidney Gilliat and Val Valentine and was "inspired by the original drawings of the girls and staff of St.Trinian's" by Ronald Searle. Whilst it's certainly ragged in construction and weak towards the end, it is nonetheless frequently hilarious. Frank Launder directs with lots of energy, as if he's trying to cover up the rough and ready storyline. Glowingly photographed by Gerald Gibbs.

CAST: George Cole, Joyce Grenfell, Lionel Jeffries; Terry-Thomas; Thorley Walters, Lloyd Lamble; Richard Wattis Alastair Sim "Returns briefly as Miss Fritton" (cameo); Eric Barker; Sabrina (non speaking cameo - a big TV star of the time); Peter Jones; Terry Scott; Kenneth Griffith; Cyril Chamberlain; Michael Ripper; Judith Furse; Ferdy Mayne; Bill Shine; Dilys Laye; Rosalind Knight; Lisa Gastoni; Charles Lloyd Pack; Wensley Pithey; Guido Lorraine; Raymond Rollett; Alma Taylor. Also others. UNBILLED CAST: Joe Robinson.

PRODUCTION COMPANY–ORIGINAL UK DISTRIBUTOR:

Sidney Gilliat-Frank Launder/John Harvel Productions - British Lion

AVAILABLE ON DVD

FILM STUDIO: Shepperton

LOCATIONS: All Nations College Easneye, Stanstead Abbotts; Littleton House, Shepperton (close ups of school)

CIRCUIT AND APPROXIMATE RELEASE DATE:

Odeon – February 1958 - Cert U - Supported by “Raiders Of Old California” (US “B” Western). In the top fourteen box office hits of the year.

RUNNING TIME ON TV: 82 minutes

FORMAT: Black and White

IN THE UK AROUND THE TIME OF RELEASE

NEWS: On February 8th seven Manchester United footballers die in an air crash at Munich airport along, with eight UK sports reporters and several club officials.

POP HITS: The Story Of My Life - Michael Holliday; Magic Moments – Perry Como

POPULAR TV: Take Your Pick (quiz series, ITV); The Army Game (sitcom, ITV)

POPULAR NEW CARS: Morris Minor (1948–1971); Vauxhall Cresta (PA) (1957–1962)

THE CAPTAIN'S TABLE (1959)

RATING: **

SYNOPSIS: A Captain is rewarded after keeping afloat a number of old cargo ships, the latest of which exploded. He is appointed Captain of a luxury cruise ship bound for Australia and if he's successful the position will be permanent. Unbeknown to him, the crew are involved in a racket "diverting" the ship's supplies. He finds himself socially awkward with situations he encounters.

REVIEW: This is one of the best British comedies of the 1950's, it's witty, insightful and fun. It's worth seeing just for the excellent cast alone. The stand-outs being John Gregson, Donald Sinden, Reginald Beckwith, Miles Malleson, Maurice Denham and Bill Kerr. The script was by John Whiting, Bryan Forbes and Nicholas Phipps (who also appears as a writer) and based on a novel by Richard "Doctor Series" Gordon. It's crammed full of good gags, makes you care about the characters and displays remarkable perception too. Jack Lee directs breezily and with tongue in cheek and injects flair and affection. A comedy of embarrassment, full of period charm and a pleasing atmosphere. Gregson's faltering attempts to be sociable are both touching and hilarious. Lots more fun than "Carry On Cruising".

CAST: John Gregson; Donald Sinden; Peggy Cummins; Nadia Gary; Reginald Beckwith; Richard Wattis; Maurice Denham; Joan Sims; Miles Malleson; Bill Kerr; Nicholas Phipps; June Jago; John Le Mesurier; Lionel Murton; James Hayter; Nora Nicholson; Harry Locke; Joseph Tomelty; Ed Devereux; John Warner; Donald Churchill; Rosalie Ashley; Beth Rogan; Lynne Cole; Yvonne Buckingham. UNBILLED CAST: Oliver Reed (extra); Michael Blakemore; Steven Berkoff; Sam Kydd; Harold Goodwin; Roland Curram; Arthur Lovegrove; Totti Truman-Taylor. Many others.

PRODUCTION COMPANY–UK DISTRIBUTOR:

The Rank Organisation/Joseph Janni/Jack Lee - Rank Film Distributors

AVAILABLE ON DVD

FILM STUDIO: Pinewood

CIRCUIT AND APPROXIMATE RELEASE DATE:

Odeon - January 1959 – Cert A - Supported by "Girl In The Woods" (US "B" film)

RUNNING TIME ON TV: 86 minutes

FORMAT: Eastmancolor

IN THE UK AROUND THE TIME OF RELEASE

NEWS: In late January there was the worst fog in many years, which brought transport chaos.

POP HITS: The Day The Rains Came – Jane Morgan; One Night and I Got Stung - Elvis Presley

POPULAR TV: Wagon Train (US western series, ITV); The Army Game (sitcom, ITV)

POPULAR NEW CARS: Ford Consul (Mk II) (1956–1962); Volkswagen (Beetle 1200) (1957–1968)

CARRY ON SERGEANT (1958)

RATING: *

SYNOPSIS: At his wedding, the groom discovers that a 28 day extension to his call up for National Service has not been applied for. As a result he has to report immediately to an army barracks for training, thus missing his honeymoon. Unbeknown to him, the training Sergeant is involved in a bet, he will win £50 if his squad passes out as the best unit. Meanwhile, his new wife gets a job in the barracks canteen. Training begins and the bunch of raw recruits doesn't exactly look promising.

REVIEW: The first "Carry On" and it would have been the last, but it rang the box office bell and soon a sequel was planned, the rest to use the cliché, is history. It's still the best, despite being little more than a series of comic situations stuck together. It has a charming innocence and a rich period air, which complements the humour. Seen in fine form here is William Hartnell as a Sergeant, five years before his most famous role as BBC TV's first Dr Who. He had played many similar roles in films before and looks like he had been playing the part all of his life! Also impressing are Kenneth Connor, Kenneth Williams, Charles Hawtrey and Eric Barker. The script was by Norman Hudis, with additional material by John Antrobus and was based on R.F. Delderfield's stage play "The Bull Boys". It's a good natured affair with a dozen or so very funny sequences and a splendidly upbeat tone. Gerald Thomas directs snappily and keeps things moving, despite the rough and ready nature of the material. Very likeable and easy to take, with virtually no low spots. Good photography by Peter Hennessy.

CAST: William Hartnell; Kenneth Connor; Kenneth Williams; Charles Hawtrey; Bob Monkhouse; Eric Barker; Shirley Eaton; Dora Bryan; Bill Owen; Hattie Jacques; Gerald Campion; Terence Longdon; Norman Rossington; Terry Scott; Ed Devereux;

Jack Smethurst; Cyril Chamberlain; James Villiers; Basil Dignam; Martin Boddey; Frank Forsyth; Anthony Sagar; Ian Whittaker; Arnold Diamond; Leigh Madison; Alec Bregonzi; Don McCorkindale; Ronald Clarke. Also others.

PRODUCTION COMPANY–ORIGINAL UK DISTRIBUTOR:

Nat Cohen and Stuart Levy/Peter Rogers - Anglo Amalgamated Film Distributors

AVAILABLE ON DVD

FILM STUDIO: Pinewood

LOCATIONS: The Queens Barracks, Stoughton, near Guildford, Surrey; the church at the start is in Beaconsfield, Buckinghamshire

CIRCUIT AND APPROXIMATE RELEASE DATE:

ABC – October 1958 - Cert U – In the top ten box office hits of the year.

RUNNING TIME ON TV: 80 minutes

FORMAT: Black and White

IN THE UK AROUND THE TIME OF RELEASE

NEWS: The Comet Aircraft flown by BOAC (British Overseas Airways Corporation) is the first jet service over the Atlantic.

POP HITS: Carolina Moon and Stupid Cupid - Connie Francis; It's All In The Game –Tommy Edwards

POPULAR TV: Wagon Train (US western series, ITV); The Army Game (sitcom, ITV)

POPULAR NEW CARS: Morris Oxford (III) (1956–1959); Singer Gazelle (II And III) (1957–1959)

CLASH BY NIGHT (1963) ("B")

RATING: **

SYNOPSIS: Two crooks approach and bribe a vehicle hire driver with £100 and he then replaces the regular driver transporting convicts to a prison. However, the new plan is to drive the coach to a barn instead of a prison. The barn roof is soaked with paraffin and if anyone breaks out to warn the police, it will be set alight. One prisoner is driven away by the crooks and a warden is shot dead when he recognises one of the abductors. The rest of them are trapped while fireworks (it's November 5th) may land on the roof.

REVIEW: A better than usual British "B" picture, made shortly before these second features ceased production. Maurice J Wilson and Montgomery Tully wrote the script and based it on a novel by Rupert Croft-Cooke. It's basically simple minded, but has some nice twists and an agreeable innocence. Tully also directed and does a lazily assured job helped by Geoffrey Faithfull's nicely lit photography. A good cast boosts things and it's different, likeable and easy to take.

CAST: Terence Longdon; Harry Fowler; Alan Wheatley; Peter Sallis; Jennifer Jayne; Vanda Godsell; Arthur Lovegrove; Mark Dignam; Robert Brown; John Arnatt; Hilda Fenemore; Stanley Meadows; Tom Bowman; Richard Carpenter; Ray Austen (Austin). UNBILLED CAST: William Simons.

PRODUCTION COMPANY–ORIGINAL UK DISTRIBUTOR:

Eternal Films - Grand National

AVAILABLE ON DVD

FILM STUDIO: Metro - Goldwyn - Mayer Studios Borehamwood

CIRCUIT AND APPROXIMATE RELEASE DATE:

ABC – December 1963 – Cert A

RUNNING TIME ON TV: 72 minutes

FORMAT: Black and White

NOTE: One of the prison guards is played by Richard Carpenter who wrote the famous cult children's TV series "Catweazle" in the 1970's.

IN THE UK AROUND THE TIME OF RELEASE

NEWS: BBC television's science fiction programme Dr Who features the first series with the Daleks.

POP HITS: She Loves You – The Beatles; You'll Never Walk Alone – Gerry and the Pacemakers

POPULAR TV: Coronation Street (ITV); Take Your Pick (quiz series, ITV)

POPULAR NEW CARS: Austin A60 Cambridge (1961–1969); Ford Zephyr 3 Mark 4 (1962–1966)

THE COCKLESHELL HEROES (1955)

RATING: **

SYNOPSIS: In 1942, a Royal Marines Captain meets his new commanding officer, a Major, at a barracks in Portsmouth. They discuss a plan to send men in canoes to plant explosives on the sides of Nazi ships near Bordeaux, France. A group of Marine volunteers then undertake an initiative test and eight are chosen for intensive training. Meanwhile the Captain and the Major have serious conflicts with each other.

REVIEW: A superior British war film, generally lively and likeable though uneven and with a strangely flat climactic last half hour. It was taken from a story by George Kent and the script was written by Bryan Forbes and Richard Maibaum, very loosely basing it on actual events. Whilst a bit lumpy, it has a dozen or so great scenes and shows lots of good humour and some intelligence. José Ferrer directs in a generally punchy and confident manner and manages a number of well staged action sequences. In front of the camera he's easily out-acted by the reliable Trevor Howard, who turns in a solid and dignified performance. Amiable supporting performances also help notably Victor Maddern, excellent as ever. Virtually continuous location sequences help a lot too as does the fine Technicolor photography of John Wilcox and Ted Moore. An energetic score, sometimes too strident, however is another plus point. John Addison provided most of the music with F Vivian Dunn credited with the engaging "Cockleshell Heroes March". An entertaining, involving and lively movie.

CAST: Jose Ferrer; Trevor Howard; Anthony Newley; Victor Maddern; David Lodge; Dora Bryan (voice dubbed by another actress); Percy Herbert; Peter Arne; Beatrice Campbell; John Van Eyssen; Robert Desmond; Christopher Lee; Sydney Tafler; Walter Fitzgerald (voice dubbed by another actor); Karel Stepanek; John

Fabian; Patrick Doonan; Andreas Malandrinos; Jacques Brunius. UNBILLED CAST: John Blythe; Sam Kydd; Graham Stewart; Pat McGrath.; Yana.

PRODUCTION COMPANY–UK DISTRIBUTOR:

Warwick Film Productions/Columbia British – Columbia

AVAILABLE ON DVD

FILM STUDIO: Shepperton

LOCATIONS: Southsea Barracks, Hampshire; Shepperton area, Middlesex; Portugal

CIRCUIT AND APPROXIMATE RELEASE DATE:

Odeon - January 1956 – Cert U - Supported by "The Crooked Web" (US "B" film)

RUNNING TIME ON TV: 96 minutes

FORMAT: Technicolor

IN THE UK AROUND THE TIME OF RELEASE

NEWS: Heroin possession becomes illegal for the first time.

POP HITS: Rock Around The Clock - Bill Haley and his Comets; Christmas Alphabet – Dickie Valentine

POPULAR TV: The Adventures of Robin Rood (ITV); Take Your Pick (quiz series, ITV)

POPULAR NEW CARS: Triumph TR3 (1955–1961); Morris Oxford (1954–1960)

CONFLICT OF WINGS (1954)

RATING: *

SYNOPSIS: A young woman visits a boat builder and learns that a highly regarded bird sanctuary is to be used for an RAF rocket range. Together with some local residents, she attempts to stop the proposal. Her boyfriend, an RAF Corporal, then faces conflicting loyalties.

REVIEW: This is possibly the best film made by the short lived government backed "Group 3" set up. Lots of refreshing location sequences shot in colour offset the fact that as a whole this is a self conscious and thin drama. Based on a novel by Don Sharp, the script was by John Pudney and Sharp and is sincere and warm hearted, yet slackly constructed and with sketchy characterisation. John Eldridge directs with much affection, but struggles with the fact that there is little to get a grip on here. Does have a winning charm to get it by.

CAST: John Gregson; Muriel Pavlow; Kieron Moore; Niall MacGinnis; Harry Fowler; Guy Middleton; Sheila Sweet; Campbell Singer; Frederick Piper; George Woodbridge; Russell Napier; William Mervyn (dual role); Charles Lloyd Pack; Bartlett Mullins; Edwin Richfield; Margaret Withers; Humphrey Lestocq; Guy Verney; Barbara Hicks; Peter Swanwick; Harold Siddons; Hugh Moxey; Tony Doonan; Beryl Cooke. Also others.

PRODUCTION COMPANY–ORIGINAL UK DISTRIBUTOR:

Group 3 - British Lion

AVAILABLE ON DVD

FILM STUDIO: Beaconsfield

LOCATIONS: RAF Leconfield, Yorkshire. Cley Mill and Ludham, both Norfolk

CIRCUIT AND APPROXIMATE RELEASE DATE:

Gaumont - April 1954 – Cert U – Supported by "Geraldine"

RUNNING TIME ON TV: 81 minutes

FORMAT: Eastmancolor

IN THE UK AROUND THE TIME OF RELEASE

NEWS: The first episode of Britain's original TV soap opera "The Grove Family" is broadcast.

POPULAR NEW CARS: Morris Minor (Series 2) (1952–1956); Humber Super Snipe Mark IV (1952–1958)

DAD'S ARMY (1971)

RATING: *

SYNOPSIS: In April 1940, after listening to a speech by Anthony Eden, the Secretary of State for War, the gruff manager of a bank in a small Kent coastal town appoints himself commander of the Local Defence Volunteers, known as "The Home Guard". Subsequently his chief cashier, an undertaker, a bank clerk and a butcher, amongst others sign up for the LDV. Patrol duties and training then begin.

REVIEW: Cinema films based on British TV sitcoms were churned out in the early to mid 1970's and most were dire. This is actually an improvement on the legendary BBC series which ran from 1968–1977. The familiar cast is the best thing here, with Arthur Lowe, John Laurie and James Beck (1929–1973) as Private Walker particularly amusing. Jimmy Perry and David Croft wrote the script, based on an idea by Perry, just as they did on TV. It's a little bitty, but jolly and cosily nostalgic and has a dozen very funny scenes. Norman Cohen directs with affection and laid back confidence and uses the many location sequences to full advantage. Of course it's somewhat silly seeing grown men act like children, but that was why it was so successful.

CAST: Arthur Lowe; John Le Mesurier; Clive Dunn; John Laurie; James Beck; Ian Lavender; Arnold Ridley; Bill Pertwee; Liz Fraser; Frank Williams; Edward Sinclair; Bernard Archard; Derek Newark; Pat Coombes; Michael Knowles; Sam Kydd (voice dubbed by another actor); Anthony Sagar; Fred Griffiths; Robert Raglan; John Baskcomb; Dervis Ward; Colin Bean; Roger Maxwell; Paul Dawkins; John D Collins; George Roubicek; the voice of Alvar Lidell as the newscaster. Also others.

PRODUCTION COMPANY–ORIGINAL UK DISTRIBUTOR:

Columbia (British) Productions/Norcon - Columbia.

AVAILABLE ON DVD

FILM STUDIO: Shepperton

LOCATIONS: Chalfont St Giles, Buckinghamshire; Cookham, Berkshire

CIRCUIT AND APPROXIMATE RELEASE DATE:

Odeon - March 1971 - Cert U – Supported by various films

RUNNING TIME ON TV: 90 minutes

FORMAT: Technicolor

IN THE UK AROUND THE TIME OF RELEASE

NEWS: The Industrial Relations Act resulted in strikes.

POP HITS: Baby Jump – Mungo Jerry; Another Day – Paul McCartney

POPULAR TV: A Family At War (drama series, ITV); Dixon Of Dock Green (police drama series, BBC)

POPULAR NEW CARS: Saab 95/96 (V4) (1967–1980); Ford Capri (1969–1974)

THE DAM BUSTERS (1955)

RATING: *

SYNOPSIS: In the spring of 1942, a doctor visits the country home of Barnes Wallis, who's the inventor of the Wellington bomber and works for Vickers Aviation. His latest idea is for "bouncing bombs" which could destroy dams in Germany's Ruhr Valley and thus flood steel factories used for war supply production. A number of trials later begin and after some setbacks, Prime Minister Winston Churchill approves the project. A special new RAF squadron at Scampton, Lincolnshire is formed, headed by Wing Commander Guy Gibson and low level flying training starts.

REVIEW: An absorbing semi-documentary style film which has achieved legendary status. It was based on Paul Brickhill's book and Guy Gibson's account of the raid "Enemy Coast Ahead". The script by R.C. Sherriff is quietly intelligent and is also very likeable and unshowy. Michael Anderson directs solidly and often with flair, managing lots of engaging location scenes. It's worth seeing for Michael Redgrave as Barnes Wallis, an over-rated, often dull actor, here he's splendidly touching and convincing. Surely this is his best film performance, he quietly out-acts a sober and to the point Richard Todd as Gibson, but he's good too. Also boosting things is the score by Leighton Lucas and the superb "The Dam Busters March" by Eric Coates. NB the actual raid sequences in the last third are disappointing and feature some jarringly obvious models and poor special effects work.

CAST: Michael Redgrave; Richard Todd; Ursula Jeans; Derek Farr; Patrick Barr; Ernest Clark; Raymond; Huntley; George Baker; John Fraser; Basil Sydney; Richard Leech; Robert Shaw; Nigel Stock; Bill Kerr; Gerald Harper; Laurence Naismith; Hugh Manning; Harold Goodwin; Arthur Howard; Richard Thorp; Charles Carson; Tim Turner; Ewen Solon; Colin Tapley; Harold

Siddons; Frederick Leister; Brian Nissen; Brewster Mason; Hugh Moxey; Edwin Styles; Stanley Van Beers; Peter Assinder; Frank Phillips. Also others. UNBILLED CAST: Peter Arne; Patrick McGoohan (a guard at a meeting); Lloyd Lamble; Edwin Richfield; the voice of John Snagge.

PRODUCTION COMPANY–ORIGINAL UK DISTRIBUTOR:

Associated British Picture Corporation – Associated British-Pathe

AVAILABLE ON DVD

FILM STUDIO: Associated British Studios Elstree

LOCATIONS: RAF Scampton, Lincolnshire; reservoirs in the Peak District, Derbyshire. Also Dorset.

CIRCUIT AND APPROXIMATE RELEASE DATE:

ABC - August 1955 – Cert U - Re-released seven weeks later. Top box office hit of the year.

RUNNING TIME ON TV: 119 minutes

FORMAT: Black and White

IN THE UK AROUND THE TIME OF RELEASE

NEWS: The Guinness Book of Records is first published.

POP HITS: Rose Marie – Slim Whitman; Dreamboat – Alma Cogan

POPULAR NEW CARS: Singer Gazelle (1955–1967); Humber Hawk (Mk VI) (1954–1957)

A DAY TO REMEMBER (1953)

RATING: **

SYNOPSIS: At a London pub, "The Hand and Flower", the regulars discuss the annual darts team outing to France. The next day, eight of them travel by ferry to Boulogne. One visits a war graves cemetery where a soldier friend is buried and then goes to a local farm where he stayed during the war. He meets the farmer's daughter who he knew from that time and romance ensues. Meanwhile the other darts players concentrate on drinking, but one or two have secret problems.

REVIEW: A pleasant, easy to take comedy drama helped by an amiable cast. Robin Estridge's script, based on a novel by Jerrard Tickell, is somewhat self conscious and thrown together, but also warm, touching and unassuming. It's directed in a low key manner by Ralph Thomas who just lets the players get on with it. Quirky and with refreshing French locations providing a nice background, it's involving and different. With a little more substance it could have been even better.

CAST: Stanley Holloway; Donald Sinden; James Hayter; Bill Owen; Harry Fowler; Edward Chapman; Meredith Edwards; Odile Versois; Joan Rice; Theodore Bikel; Brenda De Banzie; Peter Jones; Thora Hird; Arthur Hill; Lilly Kann; Vernon Gray; Patricia Raine. UNBILLED CAST: George Coulouris; Cyril Chamberlain; Hal Osmond; Judith Furse; Deryck Guyler; Shirley Eaton; Harold Lang; Fred Griffiths; Peggyann Clifford; Marianne Stone; Jacques Cey.

PRODUCTION COMPANY-ORIGINAL UK DISTRIBUTOR:

The J Arthur Rank Organisation/Betty E Box/Group Film Productions – General Film Distributors

AVAILABLE ON DVD

FILM STUDIO: Pinewood

LOCATIONS: Boulogne

CIRCUIT AND APPROXIMATE RELEASE DATE:

Gaumont - December - 1953 – Cert U - Double bill, supported by "Column South" (US western with Audie Murphy)

RUNNING TIME ON TV: 86 minutes

FORMAT: Black and White

IN THE UK AROUND THE TIME OF RELEASE

NEWS: The Piltdown man skeleton discovered in 1912 and regarded as a missing link in human development is exposed as a hoax. Big scandal!

POP HITS: Answer Me - Frankie Laine; Answer Me - David Whitfield

POPULAR NEW CARS: Austin A70 Hereford (1950–1954); Ford Zephyr (Mk I) (1950–1956)

DEAD OF NIGHT (1945)

RATING: **

SYNOPSIS: A middle aged architect drives to a house in the Kent countryside and meets a number of guests who are staying there. He has a strange feeling that he has been there before. One of the guests, a motor racing driver then tells of the supernatural experience that he's encountered. The other guests subsequently have their own spooky tales to tell.

REVIEW: A very atmospheric compendium story film, enormously helped by Michael Relph's claustrophobic art direction. John Baines and Angus MacPhail provided the script, with additional dialogue by T.E.B. Clarke. After the scene setting, it's divided into five separate stories, the first "The Hearse Driver", based on a story by E.F. Benson and directed by Basil Dearden is the best, and it's punchy and chilling. Next is "The Christmas Party", based on a story by MacPhail, and directed by (Alberto) Cavalcanti, this is low key and melancholy. Following that is "The Haunted Mirror", directed by Dearden again, is very scary and stylish too. The fourth is a comic one, "Golfing Story" directed by Charles Crichton and based on story by H.G. Wells. It's a bit absurd, but also sad. Finally Cavalcanti directs "The Ventriloquist's Dummy", this is the most highly regarded story, but it's heavily done and unpleasant.

CAST: Mervyn Johns; Roland Culver; Frederick Valk; Mary Merrall; Renee Gadd "The Hearse Driver": Judy Kelly; Anthony Baird; Miles Malleson; Robert Wyndham. "The Christmas Party": Sally Ann Howes; Michael Allan. "The Haunted Mirror": Googie Withers; Ralph Michael; Esme Percy. "Golfing Story": Basil Radford; Naunton Wayne; Peggy Bryan. "The Ventriloquist's Dummy": Michael Redgrave; Hartley Power; Garry Marsh; Elisabeth Welch; Magda Kun; Allan Jeayes.

PRODUCTION COMPANY–ORIGINAL UK DISTRIBUTOR:

Ealing Studios – Eagle-Lion Film Distributors

AVAILABLE ON DVD

FILM STUDIO: Ealing

LOCATIONS: Stoke Poges and Turville, both Buckinghamshire (Golfing Story)

CIRCUIT AND APPROXIMATE RELEASE DATE:

Gaumont - September 1945 – Cert A – Supported by "The Bullfighters" (US "B" film with Laurel and Hardy)

RUNNING TIME ON TV: 98 minutes

FORMAT: Black and White

IN THE UK AROUND THE TIME OF RELEASE

NEWS: Wartime press censorship ends.

POPULAR NEW CARS: Ford Prefect (1938–1953); Wolseley 18/85 (1938–1948)

THE DEVIL RIDES OUT (1968)

RATING: **

SYNOPSIS: In England in the 1920's, the friend of a French Duke becomes involved with devil worshippers; the Duke abducts him for his own protection. However he is influenced by the immense power of an evil Satanist priest and is drawn from the house in a trance like state.

REVIEW: The best Hammer horror of the 1960's, a different, atmospheric and tense tale which avoids too much corn. Richard Matheson's script based on the novel by Dennis Wheatley, is unexpectedly bright and clever. It's also crammed full of chilling scenes and is actually quite convincing. Terence Fisher directs far better than is usual for him and drives this along with assurance and energy. As for the cast, Christopher Lee is seen in absolute top form and plays (for a Hammer appearance) a rare good guy role. With its creepy atmosphere and un-nerving, hard edged quality it's a splendid tale of good versus evil. Fine work from James Bernard (music score); Bernard Robinson (supervising art director) and Arthur Grant (Technicolor photography).

CAST: Christopher Lee; Charles Gray; Patrick Mower; Nike Arrighi; Paul Eddington; Leon Green (voice dubbed by Patrick Allen); Sarah Lawson; Gwen Ffrangcon Davies; Rosalind Landor; Russell Waters.

PRODUCTION COMPANY–ORIGINAL UK DISTRIBUTOR:

Hammer Film Productions - Warner-Pathe

AVAILABLE ON DVD

FILM STUDIO: The Elstree Studios of Associated British Picture Corporation

LOCATIONS: Black Park, Iver, Buckinghamshire; Edgewarebury Hotel, Elstree, Hertfordshire

CIRCUIT AND APPROXIMATE RELEASE DATE:

ABC - July 1968 – Cert X - Double bill supported by "Slave Girls" (also a Hammer production).

RUNNING TIME ON TV: 91 minutes

FORMAT: Technicolor

IN THE UK AROUND THE TIME OF RELEASE

NEWS: Dad's Army makes its television debut (in black and white).

POP HITS: Baby Come Back – The Equals; I Pretend – Des O'Connor

POPULAR TV: News At Ten (ITV); Coronation Street (ITV)

POPULAR NEW CARS: Volvo 131/132 (1961–1970); Saab 95/96 (V4) (1967–1980)

DOCTOR IN LOVE (1960)

RATING: ***

SYNOPSIS: At a London hospital, a doctor becomes ill and is diagnosed with yellow jaundice. He reluctantly becomes a patient and falls for a nurse, but she's involved with other patients and runs away with one. After being discharged from hospital, he spends time at a common cold research unit with a friend, another doctor. He then starts as a GP in a country town, many mishaps follow.

REVIEW: A strangely under-rated entry in the "Doctor" series which began in 1954, this is actually the best one. It's an always pleasant, frequently very funny comedy with a lively air. The script by Nicholas Phipps (who also appears as a GP) was based on the novel by Richard Gordon and is neat and wryly amusing. There's also snappy and assured direction from Ralph Thomas who lets this coast along agreeably. Of the cast top billed Michael Craig is better than usual and seen in top form are James Robertson Justice, Leslie Phillips, Irene Handl, Ronnie Stevens (hilarious as a patient) and Reginald Beckwith. A piece of amiable popular British cinema which has an appealing period air. Splendidly photographed in Eastmancolor by Ernest Steward.

CAST: Michael Craig; Leslie Phillips; Virginia Maskell (1936–1968); James Robertson Justice; Irene Handl, Ronnie Stevens; Reginald Beckwith; Carole Lesley (1935–1974); Liz Fraser; Joan Sims; Nicholas Parsons; Nicholas Phipps; Moira Redmond; Fenella Fielding; John Le Mesurier; Michael Ward; Ambrosine Phillpotts; Meredith Edwards. UNBILLED CAST: Esma Cannon (very funny in a tiny role); Bill Fraser; Norman Rossington; Patrick Cargill; Sheila Hancock; Joan Hickson Peter Sallis; Jimmy Thompson; Charles Lloyd Pack; Avis Bunnage; John Blythe; Robin Ray; Marianne Stone; Rosalind Knight; Donald Churchill; Fred Griffiths; Roland Curram; Cyril Chamberlain; Derek Blomfield; Ernest Butcher.

PRODUCTION COMPANY–ORIGINAL UK DISTRIBUTOR:

The Rank Organisation Film Productions/Betty E Box – Rank Film Distributors

AVAILABLE ON DVD

FILM STUDIO: Pinewood

LOCATIONS: Beaconsfield, Buckinghamshire (GP Surgery)

CIRCUIT AND APPROXIMATE RELEASE DATE:

Odeon - September 1960 – Cert A – Supported by "Oklahoma Territory" (US "B" western)

RUNNING TIME TV: 93 minutes

FORMAT: Eastmancolor

NOTE: The top box office attraction in Britain in 1960.

IN THE UK AROUND THE TIME OF RELEASE

NEWS: Traffic wardens were introduced in London.

POP HITS: Apache - The Shadows; Tell Laura I Love Her - Ricky Valance

POPULAR TV: Rawhide (US western series with Clint Eastwood, ITV); No Hiding Place (crime drama series, ITV)

POPULAR NEW CARS: Austin A40 (1958–1961); Ford Anglia 105e (1959–1968)

DRY ROT (1956)

RATING: *

SYNOPSIS: At a race course, a bookmaker and his assistant have to make a quick exit when their funds won't cover a big win by a punter. They buy a horse which resembles a successful French racehorse and then plot to substitute it in a race, backing it to lose, thus making a lot of money. After employing a young Canadian as their secretary they all go to stay at a country hotel and numerous complications follow.

REVIEW: A cheerfully daft farce with silliness laid on with a spade, there's no chance of subtlety here. The script by John Roy Chapman was based on his successful stage play, which ran in the West End from 1954–1958. Maurice Elvey directs it all frantically as if to try to disguise the fact that it's basically just loads of gags stuck together. Here Ronald Shiner is seen in top form, it's forgotten that he was a big film star in the 1950's, although most of the movies he made were dreadful. Brian Rix and especially Joan Sims are fun in support. Becomes a bit much with its constant jokiness, but it's hard to dislike.

CAST: Ronald Shiner; Brian Rix; Sid James; Joan Sims; Peggy Mount; Lee Patterson; Heather Sears; Michael Shepley; Joan Haythorne; Miles Malleson; Christian Duvaleix; Wilfrid Brambell; Joan Benham; Fred Griffiths; John (Roy) Chapman (as "Claude" at the beginning); Raymond Glendenning (race commentator); John Pike; Frenchie of Stocklands (the horse). UNBILLED CAST: Shirley Ann Field.

PRODUCTION COMPANY–ORIGINAL UK DISTRIBUTOR:

Romulus/Remus - Independent Film Distributors

AVAILABLE ON DVD

FILM STUDIO: Shepperton

LOCATIONS: Kempton Park Racecourse, Surrey

CIRCUIT AND APPROXIMATE RELEASE DATE:

Gaumont - December 1956 - Cert U – Supported by "Affair in Reno" (US "B" film)

RUNNING TIME ON TV: 82 minutes

FORMAT: Black and White

NOTE: Ronald Shiner ran a pub "The Blackboys Inn" in Blackboys, Sussex from 1954.

IN THE UK AROUND THE TIME OF RELEASE

NEWS: The withdrawal of military forces from the Suez Canal begins.

POP HITS: Just Walking in the Rain – Johnnie Ray; Singing The Blues -Tommy Steele and the Steelmen

POPULAR TV: Dragnet (US crime series, ITV); Take Your Pick (quiz series, ITV)

POPULAR NEW CARS: Standard 10 (1954–1961); Renault 4 CV (1947–1961)

THE FAST LADY (1962)

RATING: ***

SYNOPSIS: Whilst out with his cycling club, a town clerk's assistant crashes his bicycle, after an altercation with a Rolls Royce. He traces the bad tempered owner and meets his young daughter. She gives him a lift home and declares her love for sports cars, after seeing a 1927 Bentley Convertible which has been brought home by a car salesman who lives in the same house. The salesman tries to persuade the clerk to buy it and to take driving lessons.

REVIEW: An often wonderfully funny and fast paced tale, one of the best and most overlooked British film comedies of the 1960's. The script by Jack Davies and Henry Blyth, based on a story by Keble Howard, is splendidly constructed, solid and highly amusing. Ken Annakin directs it in a supremely assured way and injects lots of energy and flair. It's also perfectly cast with James Robertson Justice (top billed), Leslie Phillips and especially Stanley Baxter seen in absolute top form. A great many engaging location sequences are also an integral part of the appeal here. They're shot in rich Eastmancolor by Reg Wyer and help give it a marvellous period air. Crammed full of clever gags and also observant and full of warmth, it's a splendid piece of entertainment. Expertly staged car chase at the end and Norrie Paramor provided a nice score.

CAST: Stanley Baxter; Leslie Phillips; James Robertson Justice; Julie Christie, Kathleen Harrison; Guest Stars: Eric Barker, Fred Emney; "Monsewer" Eddie Gray; Raymond Baxter; Graham Hill and John Surtees. Also: Allan Cuthbertson; Dick Emery; Esma Cannon; Deryck Guyler; Clive Dunn; Terence Alexander; Gerald Campion; Danny Green; Victor Brooks; Campbell Singer; Harold Goodwin; Marianne Stone; Michael Balfour; Ann Beach; Toke Townley; Oliver Johnston; Eddie Leslie; Martin Miller. UNBILLED CAST: Bernard Cribbins; Bill Fraser.

PRODUCTION COMPANY–UK DISTRIBUTOR:

Julian Wintle-Leslie Parkyn/Independent Artists – Rank Film Distributors

AVAILABLE ON DVD

FILM STUDIO: Independent Artists Studios Beaconsfield

LOCATIONS: Beaconsfield. Amersham and Taplow, all Buckinghamshire; Watlington, Oxfordshire

CIRCUIT AND APPROXIMATE RELEASE DATE:

Odeon - February 1963 – Cert A – Supported by "Stranglehold" (GB "B" film)

RUNNING TIME ON TV: 91 minutes

FORMAT: Eastmancolor

NOTE: Justice, Baxter and Phillips made four films together from 1962–1963.

IN THE UK AROUND THE TIME OF RELEASE

NEWS: The Sunday Times is the first British newspaper to include a regular magazine.

POP HITS: The Young Ones - Cliff Richard; Let's Twist Again - Chubby Checker

POPULAR TV: Coronation Street (ITV); Steptoe and Son (sitcom, BBC)

POPULAR NEW CARS: Citroen Ami (1961–1978); Renault 4 (1961–1980)

GENEVIEVE (1953)

RATING: **

SYNOPSIS: A London barrister prepares to take part in the annual London to Brighton vintage car run in his prized 1904 Darracq car. However his wife was looking forward to spending time that week-end at a party. After some differences of opinion his wife agrees to go on the run with her husband. Also taking part is their ad agency friend in his Spyker vehicle whose latest model girlfriend and her large St Bernard dog are passengers.

REVIEW: A breezy and likeable comedy which has achieved classic status. William Rose's script is crammed full of amusing situations and lines and is actually acutely observant about relationships. Utilising a great many location sequences, Henry Cornelius directs in a fresh and snappy manner and keeps this bubbling. A splendid cast also helps a lot with top billed Dinah Sheridan) and the under-rated John Gregson particularly good. Larry Adler's memorable score and the rich Technicolor photography of Christopher Challis impress too. Still fresh, good fun and full of charm as well.

CAST: Dinah Sheridan; John Gregson; Kenneth More; Kay Kendal; "Guest Artistes": Joyce Grenfell; Leslie Mitchell. Also; Geoffrey Keen; Reginald Beckwith; Arthur Wontner. UNBILLED CAST: Michael Medwin; Edie Martin; Michael Balfour; Fred Griffiths; Stanley Escane; Lucy Griffiths; Arthur Lovegrove; Harold Siddons.

PRODUCTION COMPANY–ORIGINAL UK DISTRIBUTOR:

The J Arthur Rank Organisation/Sirius Productions - General Film Distributors

AVAILABLE ON DVD

FILM STUDIO: Pinewood

LOCATIONS: Brighton, Sussex, various in London, Buckinghamshire and Hertfordshire

CIRCUIT AND APPROXIMATE RELEASE DATE:

Gaumont - August 1953 - Cert U – Supported by "Murder At 3 a.m." (GB "B" film)

RUNNING TIME ON TV: 83 minutes

FORMAT: Technicolor

NOTE: John Gregson did not have a driving licence when he filmed this.

IN THE UK AROUND THE TIME OF RELEASE

NEWS: John Christie had recently been hanged for the murder of a number of women, now thought to total at least eight.

POP HITS: I Believe - Frankie Laine; The Song from Moulin Rouge – Mantovani

POPULAR NEW CARS: Austin A40 Somerset (1952–1954) Vauxhall Wyvern (1951–1957)

GEORDIE (1955)

RATING: **

SYNOPSIS: In a remote part of Scotland, 12 year old Geordie McTaggart hates being small, so starts a postal course in body building. At 21, he's now tall and well built and takes over the position of head game keeper for a landowner after his father dies. He takes up the sport of throwing the hammer which leads onto big things.

REVIEW: A very pleasant comedy, although it's at its best in the first hour, the scenes in Australia are awkward. Spectacular scenery helps early on and these are richly photographed in Technicolor by Wilkie Cooper (additional photography by Bob Walker). Sidney Gilliat and Frank Launder's script, based on a novel by David Walker, is mainly gentle and wryly amusing, but could have done with more substance. Frank Launder also provided the laid back direction, which complements the slight nature of the material. Lead Bill Travers is less wooden than usual and Alastair Sim is seen at his most relaxed.

CAST: Bill Travers; Alastair Sim; Raymond Huntley; Jameson Clarke; Brian Reece; Miles Malleson; Norah Gorsen; Duncan Macrae; Stanley Baxter; Francis De Wolff; Alex Mackenzie; Molly Urquhart; Michael Ripper; Jack Radcliffe; Doris Goddard; Paul Young; Anna Ferguson; Margaret Boyd. "Mr Ranshaw" as the eagle.

PRODUCTION COMPANY–ORIGINAL UK DISTRIBUTOR:

Sidney Gilliat - Frank Launder/Argonaut Films - British Lion

AVAILABLE ON DVD

FILM STUDIO: Shepperton

LOCATIONS: The Trossachs area of Scotland including Balquiddher

CIRCUIT AND APPROXIMATE RELEASE DATE:

ABC – October 1955 – Cert U

RUNNING TIME ON TV: 95 minutes

FORMAT: Technicolor

IN THE UK AROUND THE TIME OF RELEASE

NEWS: Princess Margaret calls off her marriage to Group Captain Peter Townsend. Considerable controversy was caused by the fact that he was a divorcee.

POP HITS: Rock Around The Clock – Bill Haley and His Comets; The Man From Laramie – Jimmy Young

POPULAR TV: Take Your Pick (quiz series, ITV); Sunday Night at the London Palladium (variety series, ITV)

POPULAR NEW CARS: Morris Cowley (1954–1959); Austin A30 (1951–1956)

GIDEON OF SCOTLAND YARD/GIDEON'S DAY (GB TITLE) (1958)

RATING: **

SYNOPSIS: Chief Inspector George Gideon of the Flying Squad receives a phone call, whilst having breakfast with his wife and three children. He drives to Scotland Yard and confronts a Detective Sergeant whom the caller, an informer, had accused of taking bribes. He then learns that an 18 year old woman has been murdered in Manchester and her killer is believed to be travelling to London.

REVIEW: This is just so incredibly energetic that its numerous flaws can be partly overlooked. The script was by Ealing Studios writer T.E.B. Clarke who wrote "The Blue Lamp" eight years before. It was based on the novel "Gideon's Day" by J.J. Marric, otherwise known as John Creasey. Whilst snappy, it is scrappily put together and has too many eccentric and tiresome characters. The performers are also encouraged to act way over the top. However director John Ford (yes John Ford in Britain in 1958, not in Arizona!) drives things along in a breathless, almost manic fashion, as if to try to cover up the choppy and silly goings on. Many of the cast are flattened by the corn and clichés, but somehow the great Jack Hawkins rises above them. Splendid Technicolor photography by Frederick A Young.

CAST: Jack Hawkins; Dianne Foster; Cyril Cusack; (alarmingly hammy); Andrew Ray; James Hayter; Ronald Howard; Howard Marion Crawford; Laurence Naismith; Derek Bond; "Introducing" Anna Massey. Also: Frank Lawton; Anna Lee; John Loder; Miles Malleson; Marjorie Rhodes; Michael Shepley; Michael Trubshawe;

Jack Watling; Grizelda Hervey (hysterically hammy); Henry Longhurst; Donal Donnelly; Barry Keegan; Dervis Ward; Brian Smith; Maureen Potter (painfully unfunny). Also others. UNBILLED CAST: John Le Mesurier; Robert Raglan; Richard Leech; John Charlesworth; Lucy Griffiths; Billie Whitelaw; Gordon Harris; Stuart Saunders; Alistair Hunter; John Warwick; Many others.

PRODUCTION COMPANY–ORIGINAL UK DISTRIBUTOR:

Columbia British Productions - Columbia

AVAILABLE ON DVD

FILM STUDIO: M.G.M. British Studios Borehamwood

LOCATIONS: Various in London

CIRCUIT AND APPROXIMATE RELEASE DATE:

Odeon - May 1958 - Cert A - Supported by "Going Steady" (US "B" film)

RUNNING TIME ON TV: 90 minutes

FORMAT: Technicolor

IN THE UK AROUND THE TIME OF RELEASE

NEWS: "My Fair Lady" opens at The Theatre Royal, Drury Lane starring Rex Harrison (Noel Coward turned down the role) and Julie Andrews.

POP HITS: Who's Sorry Now – Connie Francis; Whole Lotta Woman – Marvin Rainwater

POPULAR TV: Take Your Pick (quiz show, ITV); Criss Cross Quiz (ITV)

POPULAR NEW CARS: Austin A35 (1956–1962); Humber Hawk (1945–1967)

GRAND NATIONAL NIGHT (1953)

RATING: **

SYNOPSIS: The wife of a racehorse owner goes to Liverpool to watch the Grand National steeplechase. Her husband's horse wins and when she gets home she has a confrontation with him. The next day a police detective informs him that his wife has been found murdered in Liverpool. Inconsistencies then appear, as the husband claims to have been at home the whole time.

REVIEW: This film has two intriguing things going for it, the murderer admits his guilt to another character half way through and the ending has a brilliant twist. Moralists of the time would no doubt be shocked. It was based on a 1946 stage play, but has no script credit on screen, only "From the play by Dorothy and Campbell Christie". Neat, well constructed and intelligent and it becomes more and more involving and un-nerving as it unfolds. Bob McNaught directs with confidence and he handles some scenes with real flair. A typically excellent performance by Nigel Patrick and solid supporting performances are an integral part of its appeal. Atmospheric, tense and likeable, with a fine period flavour.

CAST: Nigel Patrick; Moira Lister; Beatrice Campbell; Betty Ann Davies; Michael Hordern; Noel Purcell; Colin Gordon; Gibb McLaughlin; Barry Mackay; Leslie Mitchell; Ernest Jay. UNBILLED CAST: Russell Waters; Arthur Howard; Edward Evans; George Rose; May Hallatt.

PRODUCTION COMPANY–ORIGINAL UK DISTRIBUTOR:

George Minter/Talisman (unbilled) – Renown

AVAILABLE ON DVD

FILM STUDIO: Nettlefold Studios, Walton-On-Thames

CIRCUIT AND APPROXIMATE RELEASE DATE:

Gaumont - April 1953 – Cert A - Double bill supported by "Seminole" (US western)

RUNNING TIME ON TV: 76 minutes

FORMAT: Black and White

IN THE UK AROUND THE TIME OF RELEASE

NEWS: Casino Royale - Ian Fleming's first James Bond novel is published.

POP HITS: How Much Is That Doggie In The Window – Lita Roza; I Believe - Frankie Laine

POPULAR NEW CARS: Jowett Javelin (1947–1953); Ford Consul (Mk 1) (1950–1956)

GREAT EXPECTATIONS (1946)

RATING: ***

SYNOPSIS: Around the 1820's, an orphan named Phillip Pirrip, but known as Pip is confronted by an escaped convict, whilst in a churchyard in Romney Marsh, Kent. After bringing the prisoner a metal file and a pie, he returns home to guests. Soldiers soon capture the convict and a fellow escapee. One year later Pip is sent to play at the home of an eccentric lady recluse and becomes attracted to a young girl living there, despite her cruelty towards him. Subsequently, he becomes apprenticed to his sister's husband, a blacksmith. After six years he learns that he has a rich benefactor and travels to London to become a gentleman.

REVIEW: This is probably the best film made from a novel by Charles Dickens. For about half an hour it's like a vague nightmare and then becomes more and more absorbing. A number of scenes are quite spellbinding, notably the one where the convict Magwitch meets the grown up Pip. Dickens' work was adapted for the screen by David Lean and Anthony Havelock Allen, with Kay Walsh and Cecil McGivern. Their script is neatly constructed and is warm and human, with believable and endearing characters. It's often un-nerving, but draws the viewer into its carefully recreated nineteenth century world. This is marvellously brought to life by the great John Bryan's production design and is splendidly lit by cinematographer Guy Green, both of them deservedly won Oscars for their work. Completing the atmosphere is an engaging score by Walter Goehr. It's directed with some flair by David Lean who manages many stylish sequences. At its heart is a superb performance from the reliable as oak John Mills. In support Finlay Currie and Martita Hunt are also seen in top form. An acute study of unrequited love and how there is good in even the most unlikely people.

CAST: John Mills; Valerie Hobson; Finlay Currie; Martita Hunt; Alec Guinness; Bernard Miles; Francis L Sullivan; Introducing Anthony Wager and Jean Simmons; Also: Ivor Barnard; Freda Jackson; Hay Petrie; O.B. Clarence; Torin Thatcher; Eileen Erskine; John Forrest; Everley Gregg; Edie Martin; Frank Atkinson; George Hayes. Also others.

PRODUCTION COMPANY–ORIGINAL UK DISTRIBUTOR:

J Arthur Rank/Cineguild - General Film Distributors

AVAILABLE ON DVD

FILM STUDIO: D & P Studios (Denham and Pinewood)

LOCATIONS: Kent and London

CIRCUIT AND APPROXIMATE RELEASE DATE:

Gaumont - January 1947 – Cert A

RUNNING TIME ON TV: 113 minutes

FORMAT: Black and White

NOTE: The first major film role for Alec Guinness, who went on to appear as Fagin in Oliver Twist, David Lean's next film.

QUOTE: Miss Havisham (Martita Hunt) "I know nothing of days of the week, nothing of weeks of the year".

IN THE UK AROUND THE TIME OF RELEASE

NEWS: A severe winter continued; the British coal industry was Nationalised.

POPULAR NEW CARS: Humber Hawk (Mk I) (1945–1947); Standard 12 (1945–1948)

GREEN FOR DANGER (1946)

RATING: **

SYNOPSIS: A Scotland Yard inspector recalls events which took place in 1944. After being injured by a V1 flying bomb a postman dies during an operation at a wartime emergency hospital. Subsequently, at a staff dance a nurse announces that he was murdered and she knows who the killer is and soon after she is stabbed to death. The inspector then begins an investigation.

REVIEW: A superior crime drama, which is unusually cool and stylish for this era. It always manages to look great due to Wilkie Cooper's expert photography and the evocative production design of Peter Proud. Sidney Gilliat directs with laid back assurance and he helps to give this a remarkably fresh quality. Based on a novel by Christianna Brand, the script was written by Gilliat, and Claud Gurney. Admittedly it can be a little lumpy, but is full of pleasing quirks and has perceptive qualities too. Fine performances help notably from Trevor Howard, Alastair Sim and the great Leo Genn.

CAST: Trevor Howard; Alastair Sim; Leo Genn; Sally Gray; Rosamund John; Judy Campbell; Megs Jenkins; Moore Marriott; Ronald Adam; George Woodbridge; Henry Edwards; John Rae; Frank Ling; Wendy Thompson. UNBILLED CAST: Hattie Jacques.

PRODUCTION COMPANY–ORIGINAL UK DISTRIBUTOR:

Frank Launder-Sidney Gilliat/Individual Pictures - General Film Distributors

AVAILABLE ON DVD

FILM STUDIO: Pinewood

CIRCUIT AND APPROXIMATE RELEASE DATE:

Gaumont - March 1947 - Cert A – Supported by "Detour" (US "B" film)

RUNNING TIME ON TV: 86 minutes

FORMAT: Black and White

NOTE: This production used all three of Pinewood's studio complexes.

IN THE UK AROUND THE TIME OF RELEASE

NEWS: Floods affect large parts of the country after huge snowfalls and ice.

POPULAR NEW CARS: MG TC (1945–1949); Hillman Minx (Phase I/II) (1939–1948)

THE GREEN MAN (1956)

RATING: **

SYNOPSIS: A middle aged professional assassin recalls his career highlights killing prominent, pompous figures, beginning with his headmaster. His latest target is an arrogant merchant banker/politician who he intends to bump off at a seaside hotel "The Green Man". In the meantime an enthusiastic vacuum cleaner salesman causes problems for him at the house next door.

REVIEW: A superior mid-1950's comedy, it's snappily handled and pleasingly eccentric throughout. The script by Sidney Gilliat and Frank Launder, was based on their stage play "Meet A Body". It's crammed full of wry humour and is an engaging blend of cosiness and cynicism. Robert Day (and apparently an uncredited Basil Dearden) directs with lots of energy and flair and with tongue firmly in cheek. Three splendid comic performances also help a great deal, Alastair Sim, George Cole and Terry-Thomas (who enters two thirds of the way through) are all hilarious. Unusually and delightfully amoral and it contains a dozen excellent scenes. Good photography by Gerald Gibbs.

CAST: Alastair Sim; George Cole; Terry-Thomas; Raymond Huntley; Jill Adams; Colin Gordon; Avril Angers; Eileen Moore; Dora Bryan; John Chandos; Cyril Chamberlain; Richard Wattis; Arthur Lowe; Arthur Brough; Alexander Gauge; Peter Bull; Michael Ripper; Willoughby Goddard; Lucy Griffiths; Vivien Wood; Leslie Weston; Marie Burke; Doris Yorke. UNBILLED CAST: Terence Alexander.

PRODUCTION COMPANY–UK DISTRIBUTOR:

Frank Launder-Sidney Gilliat/Grenadier Film Productions - British Lion

AVAILABLE ON DVD

FILM STUDIO: Shepperton

LOCATIONS: Weybridge, Surrey and various in London including Holborn

CIRCUIT AND APPROXIMATE RELEASE DATE:

Odeon - October 1956 – Cert A – Supported by "Every Second Counts"

RUNNING TIME ON TV: 77 minutes

FORMAT: Black and White

NOTE: Alastair Sim (1900–1976) was an unlikely, but popular star in British films until 1961.In 1958 he became involved in a very strange, now forgotten legal case. Ron Moody had provided a voice-over for cartoons featured in a series of Heinz baked beans television commercials. Sim took legal action, claiming that Moody was impersonating him, but after much deliberation, lost his case. He became the subject of jokes and the case was even adapted in an episode of the Hancock's Half Hour radio series, called "The Impressionist" from December 1959. In this, the writers Ray Galton and Alan Simpson have Tony Hancock finding out that someone is impersonating him in a series of cornflake adverts on television.

IN THE UK AROUND THE TIME OF RELEASE

NEWS: The world's first commercial nuclear power station is opened by the Queen at Calder Hall, Cumbria.

POP HITS: A Woman In Love – Frankie Laine; Lay Down Your Arms – Ann Shelton

POPULAR TV: Armchair Theatre (drama series, ITV); Dragnet (US crime series, ITV)

POPULAR NEW CARS: MG "A" (1955–1962); Vauxhall Velox (1951–1957)

GUILT IS MY SHADOW (1950)

RATING: **

SYNOPSIS: A getaway car driver escapes from the police and travels to his uncle's remote Devon farm. He reluctantly allows him to stay there, but becomes annoyed with his behaviour. The crook subsequently gets a job at a local garage and further tension ensues when his wife turns up suddenly.

REVIEW: An interesting, forgotten rural melodrama not a complete success, but strangely compelling. Ray Kellino directs with some style, although a stilted feel creeps in. He also wrote the script with Ivan Foxwell and there were "Additional Scenes" by John Gilling. It was based on a novel "You're Best Alone" by Peter Curtis. Their work is brooding, edgy and different and draws the viewer in with extensive locations helping a lot. It's always good to see the under-rated Peter Reynolds - he's here seen at his most devious and untrustworthy. Certainly a bit glum, but it presents an offbeat clash between idyllic farm life and crime. Good art direction by Holmes Paul.

CAST: Patrick Holt; Peter Reynolds; Elizabeth Sellers; Lana Morris; Esme (Esma) Cannon; Wensley Pithey; Avice Landone; Aubrey Woods; Willoughby Gray; Laurence O'Madden.

PRODUCTION COMPANY–ORIGINAL UK DISTRIBUTOR:

Associated British Picture Corporation - Associated British-Pathe

NOT AVAILABLE ON DVD

FILM STUDIO: The Elstree Studios of Associated British Picture Corporation Ltd.

LOCATIONS: Ashburton, Devon

CIRCUIT AND APPROXIMATE RELEASE DATE:

ABC - April 1950 – Cert A

RUNNING TIME ON TV: 86 minutes

FORMAT: Black and White

IN THE UK AROUND THE TIME OF RELEASE

NEWS: The Eagle comic is published for the first time.

POPULAR NEW CARS: Vauxhall Velox (1948–1951); Hillman Minx (Phase IV) (1949–1951)

HALF A SIXPENCE (1967)

RATING: *****

SYNOPSIS: In the 1890's, Arthur Kipps, a young orphan, leaves his sweetheart and goes to work in a drapery store in a Kent town. She accepts half of a sixpence coin as a token of devotion and she agrees to be "his girl" After corresponding with her for a number of years, they eventually meet up again. He then encounters a flamboyant actor, who also writes plays, and he mentions a newspaper announcement indicating that young Kipps is going to inherit money.

REVIEW: Perhaps the best and certainly the most shamefully under-rated of 1960's film musicals. It's likeable, full of life and has some great songs. In the lead role Tommy Steele was never better, he absolutely lights up the screen. He repeated his 1963 West End and 1966 Broadway stage success in the role. George Sidney directs it all with incredible flair and exuberance, aided by Gillian Lynne's first rate choreography. The splendid Technicolor photography of Geoffrey Unsworth and lovely locations impress too. The script ("Book") by Beverley Cross was based on H.G. Wells' 1905 novel "Kipps" and was adapted by Dorothy Kingsley. Their work is both warm and full of unexpected intelligence and perception and flows marvellously. The best of the superb songs are the title one, plus the famous "Flash, Bang Wallop" and especially "I'd Buy Me A Banjo" and "This Is My World". Irwin Kostal, fresh from "The Sound of Music" did a brilliant job supervising, arranging and conducting the score. Most of the songs were written by David Heneker, usually on his own. Overall a frequently delightful, always enjoyable super-musical made with breathless energy and with loads of incredible set-piece sequences. Also, if ever there was a film in which all of life's riddles are answered, this is it. It says be yourself and be wary of materialism, amongst many other things.

CAST: Tommy Steele; Julia Foster (singing voice - Marti Webb, uncredited, she played the role of Ann in the original West End stage production); Penelope Horner; Grover Dale; Elaine Taylor; Hilton Edwards; James Villiers; James Bolam; Christopher Sandford; Pamela Brown; Jean Anderson; Allan Cuthbertson; Gerald Campion; Harry Locke; Bartlett Mullins; Aleta Morrison; Julian Orchard; Norman Mitchell; Bridget Armstrong; Alistair Hunter; Queenie Watts; George Moon; Pat Ashton; Sydney Bromley; Carole Walker; Julia Sutton; Leslie Meadows; Sheila Falconer; Roy Evans; Lesley Judd (one of the dancers, who went on to be a Blue Peter presenter from 1971–1978). Also others. UNBILLED CAST: Tottie Truman-Taylor.

PRODUCTION COMPANY–ORIGINAL UK DISTRIBUTOR:

Paramount Film Service - Paramount

AVAILABLE ON DVD: US Import only (Region 1)

FILM STUDIO: Shepperton

LOCATIONS: Aylesford and Tunbridge Wells, Kent. Eastbourne, Sussex. Blenheim Palace, Oxfordshire. Oakley Court, Bray, Berkshire

CIRCUIT AND APPROXIMATE RELEASE DATE:

ABC - December 1968 - Cert U

RUNNING TIME ON TV: 146 minutes

FORMAT: Technicolor

NOTE: "Kipps" was filmed as a straight drama in 1941 starring Michael Redgrave. The 1967 film cost £2.5 million, a huge amount back then.

IN THE UK AROUND THE TIME OF RELEASE

NEWS: The Trades Descriptions act becomes law.

POP HITS: Lily The Pink – The Scaffold; The Good, The Bad And The Ugly - Hugo Montenegro

POPULAR TV: Coronation Street (ITV); Father Dear Father (sitcom, ITV)

POPULAR NEW CARS: Vauxhall Viva (HB) (1966–1970); Ford Escort (1968–1974)

THE HAPPIEST DAYS OF YOUR LIFE (1950)

RATING: **

SYNOPSIS: A new young English teacher arrives at a private boarding school for boys in the country. In the staff common room, the headmaster announces that he hopes to become head of a major school. As part of his application, the governors are due to study his methods. Unfortunately, due to a Ministry of Education error, over 100 girls from another school and their headmistress and teachers suddenly appear. Chaos ensues.

REVIEW: The splendid cast is the best thing about this rather contrived farce. Seen in fine form, Alastair Sim, Margaret Rutherford, Joyce Grenfell, Guy Middleton and Richard Wattis rise well above the obvious situations. It was based on the 1948 Apollo Theatre production by John Dighton which ran for 605 performances with Rutherford starring. The script here was written by Frank Launder and Dighton and has a dozen or so wonderful scenes, but a number are flat. Launder also directed and does a confident, tongue in cheek job. He's ably assisted by Stan Pavey's slick photography and Josef Bato's detailed art direction. An engaging period air and some wryly amusing interchanges help it over the rough patches.

CAST: Alastair Sim; Margaret Rutherford; Joyce Grenfell; Guy Middleton; Richard Wattis; Edward Rigby; John Bentley; Bernadette O'Farrell; Muriel Aked; Gladys Henson; Arthur Howard; Laurence Naismith; Russell Waters; Percy Walsh; Harold Goodwin; John Turnbull; Stringer Davis; George Benson; Kenneth Downey; William Simons (Ventress in Heartbeat - here a schoolboy); Myrette Morven; Stanley Lemin. Also others. UNBILLED CAST: George Cole; Vi Stevens.

PRODUCTION COMPANY–UK DISTRIBUTOR:

Frank Launder-Sidney Gilliat/Individual Pictures - British Lion

AVAILABLE ON DVD

FILM STUDIO: Alliance Film Studios, London (Hammersmith)

LOCATIONS: Langley Court, Liss, Hampshire

CIRCUIT AND APPROXIMATE RELEASE DATE:

ABC - April 1950 – Cert U

RUNNING TIME ON TV: 77 minutes

FORMAT: Black and White

QUOTE: Richard Wattis: "Won't you ever grow up?" Guy Middleton: "I certainly hope not".

IN THE UK AROUND THE TIME OF RELEASE:

NEWS: An air crash at Glamorgan kills 80 of the 83 aboard; a new town at Corby in Northamptonshire is announced.

POPULAR NEW CARS: Morris Minor (Series MM) (1948–1953); Austin A40 Devon (1947–1952)

A HARD DAY'S NIGHT (1964)

RATING: **

SYNOPSIS: The Beatles pop group take a train from Liverpool to London for a television studio broadcasting session. Various encounters and incidents happen during and after their journey.

REVIEW: Simply the best film to showcase a pop group and in 1964 it was way ahead of its time. Director Richard Lester basically made amongst the first pop videos here and most of the set piece musical numbers are still pure gold. It helps that the most famous group of all time has real charisma and seem approachable and likeable. Forget Alun Owen's bitty script, which has a lot of dumb moments and looks like it was written in half an hour, just concentrate on the Fab Four and their personalities and songs. Includes the following wonderful ones: "I Should Have Known Better", "If I Fell", "All My Loving" and "Can't Buy Me Love", amongst others.

CAST: John Lennon; Paul McCartney; George Harrison; Ringo Starr; Wilfred Brambell; Norman Rossington; John Junkin; Victor Spinetti; Anna Quayle; Derek Guyler; Richard Vernon; Eddie Malin; Robin Ray; Lionel Blair; David Jason; Alison Seebohm. UNBILLED CAST: Kenneth Haigh; Michael Trubshawe; Derek Nimmo; Marianne Stone; Gordon Rollings; David Langton; John Bluthal; Margaret Nolan; Julian Holloway.

PRODUCTION COMPANY-ORIGINAL UK DISTRIBUTOR:

Walter Shenson - United Artists

AVAILABLE ON DVD

FILM STUDIO: Twickenham

LOCATIONS: Various London locations. Crowcombe, Somerset

CIRCUIT AND APPROXIMATE RELEASE DATE:

Odeon – September 1964 – Cert U – In the top fourteen box office hits of the year.

RUNNING TIME ON TV: 94 minutes

FORMAT: Black and White

IN THE UK AROUND THE TIME OF RELEASE

NEWS: Match of the Day had just begun on BBC Television.

POP HITS: You Really Got Me – The Kinks; Have I The Right - The Honeycombs

POPULAR TV: Coronation Street (ITV); No Hiding Place (crime drama series, ITV)

POPULAR CARS: Austin Mini (Mk I) (1959–1967); Ford Anglia (105E) (1959–1967)

HELL DRIVERS (1957)

RATING: **

SYNOPSIS: After a test drive, a mysterious stranger is accepted as a ballast driver, carrying heavy loads at high speeds for a road haulage company. He gets a room in a boarding house, where many of the drivers stay and visits the nearby café. He then determines to complete the most runs in a day, but an aggressive "pace setter" has other ideas.

REVIEW: Still fresh and very different from other British films of the time, this is an enjoyable blend of action and drama. It was scripted by John Kruse and C. Raker Endfield, based on a short story by Kruse and adapted for the screen by Endfield. Amazingly insightful and intelligent and it's also well constructed, tense and unpredictable. "Cy" Endfield directed too and does a very confident job, handling the action sequences with bravado and the drama equally well. Boosting him is Ernest Archer's excellent gritty art direction and Geoffrey Unsworth's first rate photography. Good playing all round adds to the convincing air, with Stanley Baker playing an outsider effectively, though Patrick McGoohan hams it up. Hubert Clifford's pounding score is another bonus here. Absorbing, snappy and fascinating for its extensive location shooting and period details.

CAST: Stanley Baker; Patrick McGoohan; Peggy Cummins; Herbert Lom; William Hartnell; Sean Connery (billed 12th); Sid James; Gordon Jackson; David McCallum; Alfie Bass; George Murcell; Wilfrid Lawson; Jill Ireland; Marjorie Rhodes; Wensley Pithey; Vera Day; Beatrice Varley; Robin Bailey; John Horsley; Marianne Stone; Jerry Stovin; John Miller; Ronald Clarke. UNBILLED CAST: Hal Osmond; Howard Pays; Vi Stevens; Harry Markham; Charles Lamb; Ian Wilson.

PRODUCTION COMPANY–ORIGINAL UK DISTRIBUTOR:

The Rank Organisation Film Productions/Aqua Film Productions - J Arthur Rank Film Distributors

AVAILABLE ON DVD

FILM STUDIO: Pinewood

LOCATIONS: Upper Beeding, Sussex; Stanwell, Middlesex. Colnbrook, Berkshire. The area around Pinewood Studios, Buckinghamshire

CIRCUIT AND APPROXIMATE RELEASE DATE:

Odeon - July 1957 – Cert A – Supported by "The Heart Within" (GB "B" film)

RUNNING TIME ON TV: 104 minutes

FORMAT: Black and White

NOTE: The tag line on one of the posters was "It was a fight to the death and the weapons were ten ton trucks".

IN THE UK AROUND THE TIME OF RELEASE

NEWS: The Medical Research Council links tobacco smoking to cancer. Prime Minister Harold Macmillan famously announces "Most of our people have never had it so good".

POP HITS: All Shook Up - Elvis Presley; Gamblin' Man plus Putting On The Style – Lonnie Donegan

POPULAR TV: Criss Cross Quiz (ITV); Emergency Ward Ten (medical drama series, ITV)

POPULAR NEW CARS: Rover 90 (P4) (1953–1959) Riley One Point Five (1957–1965)

THE HEROES OF TELEMARK (1965)

RATING: **

SYNOPSIS: In Telemark, Norway in 1942, the local Resistance unit attacks a convoy of trucks belonging to the Nazi occupiers. Reprisals follow, 15 civilians are shot dead. The Reich Commisar then demands that "heavy water" production at a local fertiliser factory is increased by 400%. Making a trip to England with a scientist, the Resistance leader is instructed by British officials to destroy the plant in order to prevent production of an atomic bomb. After being parachuted back to Norway, the two men face serious problems with their mission.

REVIEW: An agreeable, above average war film, well made and likeable. Anthony Mann directs in a cool and assured way and makes excellent use of spectacular, mainly snow covered locations. He also helps to imbue this with real tension and expertly stages numerous action sequences. The script was by Ivan Moffatt and Ben Barzman and an uncredited Harold Pinter worked on some scenes (!). Strong, gutsy performances from macho men Kirk Douglas and Richard Harris also help, as does Malcolm Arnold's rousing score. An involving "impossible mission" film based on fact, although it sometimes looks like it was influenced more by Alistair Maclean novels.

CAST: Kirk Douglas; Richard Harris; Michael Redgrave; Ulla Jacobsson; Eric Porter; David Weston; Mervyn Johns; Roy Dotrice; Anton Diffring; Barry Jones; Ralph Michael; Geoffrey Keen; Maurice Denham; Jennifer Hilary; Alan Howard; Faith Brook; Elvi Hale; Patrick Jordan; George Murcell; William Marlowe; Karel Stepanek; Russell Waters; David Davies; Gerard Heinz; Brook Williams; Wolf Frees; Philo Hauser; Grace Arnold; Victor Beaumont; John Golightly; Jan Conrad; Sebastian Breaks; Robert Bruce; Brian Jackson; Paul Hansard; Jemma Hyde; Howard Douglas.

PRODUCTION COMPANY–ORIGINAL UK DISTRIBUTOR:

The Rank Organisation Film Productions/Benton Film Productions - Rank Film Distributors

AVAILABLE ON DVD

FILM STUDIO: Pinewood (and the studio tank was used for the boat sinking scenes)

LOCATIONS: Norway

CIRCUIT AND APPROXIMATE RELEASE DATE:

Odeon - January 1966 - Cert U - Supported by "European Tapestry" (short film)

RUNNING TIME ON TV: 124 minutes

FORMAT: Eastmancolor - Panavision 70

NOTE: The tag line on one of the posters "The stakes were the highest the world has ever known".

IN THE UK AROUND THE TIME OF RELEASE:

NEWS: The pirate radio ship Radio Caroline runs aground at Frinton.

POP HITS: Keep On Running - The Spencer Davis Group; The Carnival Is Over - The Seekers

POPULAR TV: University Challenge (quiz series, ITV); The Power Game (drama series, ITV)

POPULAR NEW CARS: Morris Mini Minor (1959–1969); Reliant Regal (1962–1973)

THE HISTORY OF MR POLLY (1949)

RATING: *****

SYNOPSIS: In 1896, after six years as an assistant in a London outfitters shop, Alfred Polly gets the sack for slackness. Out of work for a long spell, he then learns that his father is ill and he subsequently dies. An inheritance of £500 follows and on a new bicycle, he tours the countryside and visits his aunt and three female cousins. A young girl he subsequently meets and falls for humiliates him and on the rebound he courts and marries one of the cousins.

REVIEW: This is one of British cinema's finest films, a strangely overlooked little gem. It has a haunting quality and depicts a lost soul who eventually finds out who he is. Anthony Pelissier's script based on H.G. Wells' 1910 novel is quite beguiling and highly intelligent - there's wisdom and insight galore here. Pelissier also directed and does a consummately stylish job, assisted by Desmond Dickinson's wonderful photography. Added to this there's an endearing performance from the superb John Mills. He shows what an incredible range he had, his pixie-like Polly is light years away from the stiff upper lip roles. Full of a rich 1900's period air, partly the work of Duncan Sutherland's expert art direction, it's a winner. A delight, witty, warm and full of thought, with at least a dozen scenes spellbindingly good. Fine score by William Alwyn.

CAST: John Mills; Sally Ann Howes; Finlay Currie; Betty Ann Davies; Edward Chapman; Megs Jenkins; Gladys Henson; Moore Marriott; Miles Malleson; Dandy Nichols; Juliet Mills (aged 7); Wally Patch; Edie Martin; David Horne; Diana Churchill; Ernest Jay; Shelagh Fraser; Lawrence Baskcomb. UNBILLED CAST: Michael Ripper; Frederick Piper; Irene Handl; Doris Hare; Ian Wilson; Cyril Smith; Cameron Hall; Lyndon Brook.

PRODUCTION COMPANY–UK DISTRIBUTOR:

J Arthur Rank/Two Cities Films/Pictor Films – General Film Distributors

AVAILABLE ON DVD

FILM STUDIO: Denham

LOCATIONS: The country pub was a set built by a river at the back of Denham studios, as no suitable "real" pub could be found.

CIRCUIT AND APPROXIMATE RELEASE DATE:

Gaumont - April 1949 - Cert A – Supported by "Kings Of The Turf"

RUNNING TIME ON TV: 92 minutes

FORMAT: Black and White

IN THE UK AROUND THE TIME OF RELEASE:

NEWS: The Royal Navy's ship HMS Amethyst evacuates Commonwealth refugees from China's Yangtze river. The incident was made into a 1957 film starring Richard Todd, "Yangtze Incident".

POPULAR NEW CARS: Ford Prefect (1938–1953); Hillman Minx (Phase III etc) (1948–1957)

HOLIDAY CAMP (1947)

RATING: ***

SYNOPSIS: Amongst the new arrivals at a seaside holiday camp are bus driver Joe Huggett and his wife, teenage son and widowed daughter, who has brought her baby. Other guests include a woman looking for romance, a sailor, a suave ex-RAF officer, a runaway couple and a lonely middle aged spinster. After settling into their chalets, various problems, encounters and romances follow.

REVIEW: This is easily the best fun of the four "Huggett" films made between 1947 and 1949. However it's at its best in the freewheeling first half, it then becomes more serious. The script was by Muriel and Sydney Box and Peter Rogers (the "Carry On" producer) with additional dialogue by Mabel and Ted Constanduros and Ted Willis. It's somewhat episodic, but is both populist and intelligent. The amazing and delightfully liberal minded attitude to, the runaway couple is a revelation here. Good characterisation helps a lot and there are great performances from Flora Robson (top billed) Jimmy Hanley and the wonderful as ever Jack Warner. It's all directed with confidence and flair by Kenneth (Ken) Annakin who injects lots of affection. Good humoured, lively and entertaining, it's one of the most under-rated British movies of the 1940's.Glowingly photographed by Jack Cox and it has an enchanting period atmosphere. A warm and human film.

CAST: Flora Robson; Jack Warner; Jimmy Hanley; Dennis Price; Hazel Court; Kathleen Harrison; Emrys Jones; Yvonne Owen; Esmond Knight; Peter Hammond; Esma Cannon; John Blythe; Susan Shaw; Maurice Denham; Beatrice Varley; Jane Hylton; Dennis Harkin; Jeanette Tregarthen; "The Holiday Camp Guest Stars" – Patricia Roc; Cheerful Charlie Chester and Gerry Wilmot. Also: Alfie Bass; Reginald Purdell; Jack Raine; Pamela Bramah; Phil Fowler; Jack Ellis; John Stone. UNBILLED CAST: Diana Dors (extra in beauty contest and "jitterbugging" with John Blythe the end)

PRODUCTION COMPANY–ORIGINAL UK DISTRIBUTOR:

J Arthur Rank/Gainsborough Pictures - General Film Distributors

AVAILABLE ON DVD (As part of the Huggetts films boxset)

FILM STUDIO: The Gainsborough Studios, London

LOCATIONS: The camp is Butlin's at Filey, North Yorkshire. The railway station is Skegness, Lincolnshire

CIRCUIT AND APPROXIMATE RELEASE DATE:

Gaumont – September 1947 – Cert A – Supported by "The Lone Wolf In Mexico" (US "B" film)

RUNNING TIME ON TV: 93 minutes

FORMAT: Black and White

NOTE: The character played by Dennis Price was roughly based on the sadistic killer Neville Heath, hanged in 1946.

IN THE UK AROUND THE TIME OF RELEASE

NEWS: The first ever Edinburgh Festival was inaugurated.

POPULAR NEW CARS: Hillman Minx (Mk 1) (1945–1947); Austin A40 Devon (1947–1952)

THE HOLLY AND THE IVY (1952)

RATING: ***

SYNOPSIS: Just before Christmas in 1948, several relatives are contacted by letter inviting them to a family gathering. They go to stay with an elderly vicar in a snow covered Norfolk rectory. Just before they all arrive, the vicar's 31 year old daughter learns that her fiancé wants to accept a dream job building an aerodrome in South America. She tells him that she cannot go with him as she has to stay to look after her father.

REVIEW: A very wise drama, which on the surface looks pretty ordinary, but there's a rare depth of feeling here. Anatole De Grunwald's script was based on Wynyard Browne's 1950 stage hit and is highly intelligent, warm and involving. There's also smooth direction from George More O'Ferrall who shows how a piece of theatre can be effectively cinematic. Excellent performances also help, with Celia Johnson, Margaret Leighton, John Gregson, Hugh Williams and Denholm Elliott stand outs. An endearing period air is an integral part of the appeal here. Splendid photography by Ted Scaife and believable sets by Vincent Korda and Frederick Pusey are worth noting too. Full of observant touches and very human.

CAST: Ralph Richardson; Celia Johnson; John Gregson; Margaret Leighton; Hugh Williams; Denholm Elliott; Robert Flemyng; William Hartnell; Maureen Delaney; Margaret Halstan; Roland Culver; Dandy Nichols; John Barry (not the composer).

PRODUCTION COMPANY–ORIGINAL UK DISTRIBUTOR:

London Films - British Lion

AVAILABLE ON DVD

FILM STUDIO: The British Lion Studio Shepperton

CIRCUIT AND APPROXIMATE RELEASE DATE:

ABC – December 1952 – Cert A

RUNNING TIME ON TV: 77 minutes

FORMAT: Black and White

NOTE: The original stage play's author Wynyard Browne (1911–1964) was the son of a vicar and subsequently co-wrote the screenplay for Hobson's Choice (1954).

IN THE UK AROUND THE TIME OF RELEASE

NEWS: The Flower Pot Men is first broadcast on BBC television.

POPULAR NEW CARS: Ford Consul (Mk I) (1950–1956); Morris Oxford (1948–1954)

HOME AT SEVEN (1952)

RATING: **

SYNOPSIS: A middle aged bank official returns home to Bromley, Kent at 7 pm one evening. He's stunned when his wife tells him that he's been missing for 24 hours and he can't explain his absence. The president of his local social club, of which he is treasurer, then informs him that £515 was stolen from the safe. The club steward claims to have seen the bank official take the money and was subsequently murdered. A police inspector then calls on him.

REVIEW: This is a wonderfully cosy crime drama with a great period atmosphere. However, it is a little stiff and shaky and could have done with a bit more substance. Anatole De Grunwald's script based on the stage play by R C Sherriff is neat and thoughtful, but not completely rounded. Recreating his stage role, Ralph Richardson turns in a suitably bewildered performance. In support Margaret Leighton, Jack Hawkins and the great Campbell Singer are all seen in fine form. Richardson also directed his first and last time in the cinema and does a proficient, unshowy job. Despite its faults, it's intriguing, ever so likeable and consistently entertaining. Obvious, but first rate exterior sets for the main house by set designers Vincent Korda and Frederick Pusey. Filmed in fifteen days!

CAST: Ralph Richardson; Margaret Leighton; Jack Hawkins; Campbell Singer; Michael Shepley; Frederick Piper; Meriel Forbes; Gerald Case; Margaret Withers; Diana Beaumont. UNBILLED CAST: Archie Duncan; Johnnie Schofield.

PRODUCTION COMPANY–ORIGINAL UK DISTRIBUTOR:

London Films - British Lion

AVAILABLE ON DVD

FILM STUDIO: The British Lion Studio Shepperton

CIRCUIT AND APPROXIMATE RELEASE DATE:

ABC - March 1952 - Cert U - Double bill Supporting "Remember That Face"

RUNNING TIME ON TV: 82 minutes

FORMAT: Black and White

IN THE UK AROUND THE TIME OF RELEASE

NEWS: Churchill reveals that Britain has an atomic bomb.

POPULAR NEW CARS: Austin A40 Somerset (1952–1954); Ford Consul (Mk 1) (1951–1956)

HUE AND CRY (1947)

RATING: **

SYNOPSIS: In London, a 15 year old boy, one of a gang of friends, is an avid comic reader. One day he suspects that his comic contains stories linked to actual crimes. A real lorry's number plate is featured in one of the stories. He tells his theory to a policeman who dismisses it, but arranges for him to get a job as a porter at a Covent Garden wholesaler. He continues his investigation, convinced that he's onto something. With a friend he pays a visit to the eccentric writer of the comic strip.

REVIEW: A lively and likeable Ealing comedy, the first in the cycle which ended in 1955 with the over-rated "The Ladykillers". It's greatly helped by lots of refreshing early post-war London location sequences, brightly photographed by Douglas Slocombe. T.E.B. Clarke's script has real momentum and is full of engaging quirks and twists. The whole thing is directed with confidence by Charles Crichton and he injects plenty of energy too. Enthusiastic playing all round adds to the fun. An atmospheric and involving tale, all wonderfully innocent.

CAST: Alastair Sim; Jack Warner; Valerie White; Jack Lambert; "The Blood and Thunder Boys"- Harry Fowler; Joan Dowling; Stanley Escane; Douglas Barr; Ian Dawson; Gerald Fox; David Simpson; Albert Hughes; John Hudson; David Knox; Jeffrey Sirett; James Crabb. Also; Frederick Piper; Vida Hope; Grace Arnold; Joey Carr; Bruce Belfrage; Paul Demel. Also others. UNBILLED CAST: Dandy Nichols.

PRODUCTION COMPANY–ORIGINAL UK DISTRIBUTOR:

J Arthur Rank/Ealing Studios - General Film Distributors

AVAILABLE ON DVD

FILM STUDIO: Ealing

LOCATIONS: Various in London including Holborn

CIRCUIT AND APPROXIMATE RELEASE DATE:

Gaumont – June 1947 – Cert U – Supported by "That Brennan Girl"

RUNNING TIME ON TV: 79 minutes

FORMAT: Black and White

IN THE UK AROUND THE TIME OF RELEASE

NEWS: School leaving age recently rose to 15.

POPULAR NEW CARS: Triumph 1800 (1946–1949); Ford V8 Pilot (1947–1951)

I WAS MONTY'S DOUBLE (1958)

RATING: ***

SYNOPSIS: In 1944 a major who works for Military Intelligence is told by his superior officer that a plan is needed to persuade the Nazis that a European invasion will not be via France. At a stage show the Major sees an actor who bears an uncanny resemblance to General Montgomery. As Montgomery is certain to lead any invasion, the actor is persuaded to impersonate him. Their plan being that if he's seen nowhere near France, the Nazis will assume that the attack will take place elsewhere.

REVIEW: An engaging and cosy "wizard wheeze", this is one of the most fun of all British war films from their golden age in the 1950's. Bryan Forbes' script is a highly adept blend of good humour, thrills and high drama. It's also well constructed and draws the viewer in at every turn. Forbes' based his screenplay on the 1954 book by the Australian M.E. (Meyrick Edward) Clifton - James (1898–1963) who here plays himself 14 years after his exploit. John Mills and Cecil Parker are the star names here and both are seen at the top of their form. It's directed with bravado by John Guillermin and the whole thing glides along agreeably. The score by John Addison, especially his main theme adds to the enjoyment here and the other production values are good too. N.B. the kidnapping attempt in the last fifteen minutes did not actually take place.

CAST: John Mills; Cecil Parker. "Introducing" M.E. Clifton James as himself. Guest Artist: Marius Goring. Also: Michael Hordern; Leslie Phillips; Bryan Forbes; Vera Day; Victor Maddern; Barbara Hicks; Sid James; James Hayter; Alfie Bass; Patrick Allen; Duncan Lamont; John Le Mesurier; Allan Cuthbertson; Ronnie Stevens; David Lodge; Harry Fowler; Marne Maitland; Macdonald Parke; Edward Judd; Anthony Sagar; Frederick Jaeger; Walter

Gotell; David Davies; Sam Kydd; Maureen Connell; Victor Beaumont; John Heller; Bill Nagy; George Eugeniou; Kenneth Warren; Brian Weske; John Gale; Martin Shaban; Desmond Roberts; Ronald Wilson. UNBILLED CAST: Ian Whittaker; Max Butterfield; Gordon Harris; Steven Berkoff.

PRODUCTION COMPANY–ORIGINAL UK DISTRIBUTOR:

Associated British Picture Corporation/Film Traders/Setfair Productions - Associated British-Pathe

AVAILABLE ON DVD

FILM STUDIO: Walton Studios, Walton On Thames

LOCATIONS: Tangiers; Gibraltar

CIRCUIT AND APPROXIMATE RELEASE DATE:

ABC - January 1959 – Cert U

RUNNING TIME ON TV: 96 minutes

FORMAT: Black and White

IN THE UK AROUND THE TIME OF RELEASE

NEWS: Dense fog causes problems at the end of January.

POP HITS: It's Only Make Believe - Conway Twitty; Hoots Mon - Lord Rockingham's XI

POPULAR TV: Spot The Tune (quiz series, ITV); TV Playhouse (drama series, ITV)

POPULAR NEW CARS: Ford Consul (Mk 2) (1956–1962); Wolseley 1500 (1957–1965)

I'M ALL RIGHT JACK (1959)

RATING: ***

SYNOPSIS: In the early 1950's, an eager, but naïve university graduate fails at interviews for several management positions. His uncle then arranges a job for him as a forklift truck driver at an armaments factory. However, his fellow workers think that he's a secret "time and motion" study expert and report him to the shop steward. Meanwhile his uncle is arranging a fiddle regarding a contract with a Middle Eastern country.

REVIEW: This is worth seeing for the cast alone, notably Peter Sellers as Fred Kite the deadly serious union official. It's possibly his funniest screen performance; he's hilarious and yet makes his character touching and likeable. Top billed Ian Carmichael is also in first rate form. typically here as a well meaning innocent. Greatly impressing too are Terry-Thomas, Irene Handl and the brilliant as ever Victor Maddern. The script was by Frank Harvey, John Boulting and Alan Hackney and based on a novel by Hackney, which is actually a bit rough and ready. However there is acute perception here, although with a bitter and cynical tone. John Boulting also directed and does a solid job and helps the marvellous players rise above the material's limitations.

CAST: Peter Sellers; Terry Thomas; Guest Stars: Richard Attenborough; Margaret Rutherford; Dennis (billed as Denis) Price. Also: Irene Handl; Victor Maddern; Liz Fraser; Miles Malleson; John Le Mesurier; Kenneth Griffith; Raymond Huntley; Marne Maitland; Malcolm Muggeridge; Sam Kydd; John Comer; Donal Donnelly; Harry Locke; John Glyn-Jones; Fred Griffiths; Basil Dignam; Ronnie Stevens; Terry Scott; Brian Oulton; Esma Cannon; David Lodge; Michael Bates; Martin Boddey; Robin Ray; Cardew Robinson; Stringer Davis; Michael Ward; Marianne Stone; Wally Patch; Alun Owen; Muriel Young; Keith Smith; Tony Comer; William Peacock; Eynon Evans; Frank Phillips (and opening narration). Many others.

PRODUCTION COMPANY–ORIGINAL UK DISTRIBUTOR:

Charter Film Productions - British Lion

AVAILABLE ON DVD

FILM STUDIO: Shepperton

LOCATIONS: Shepperton Studios as the factory

CIRCUIT AND APPROXIMATE RELEASE DATE:

Odeon – September 1959 - Cert A - Supported by "The Legend Of Tom Dooley" (US "B" film)

RUNNING TIME ON TV: 100 minutes

FORMAT: Black and White

IN THE UK AROUND THE TIME OF RELEASE

NEWS: Trunk calls were available from public call boxes in Bristol - the charges were 3d, 6d and one Shilling. The system would eventually replace the "Button A" and "Button B"units introduced in 1925.

POP HITS: Living Doll – Cliff Richard and The Drifters; Only Sixteen – Craig Douglas

POPULAR TV: Wagon Train (US western series, ITV); Emergency Ward Ten (medical drama series, ITV)

POPULAR NEW CARS: Morris Mini Minor (1959–1969); Ford Anglia (1959–1968)

INN FOR TROUBLE (1960)

RATING: ***

SYNOPSIS: A brewery worker retires after 15 years and his domineering wife then insists that he is given a pub as his leaving gift. They find that customers are in short supply, however, so they decide to find ways to attract them. The brewery subsequently receives an offer to buy their pub and is unaware that the potential purchaser, a rival brewer, knows that a motorway is planned, which would bring much more custom.

REVIEW: A decidedly under-rated and overlooked British comedy film, it's delightfully modest and full of fun. It was one of the very first cinema movie spin-offs taken from a British television comedy. Fred Robinson's script was based on characters from his TV series "The Larkins" first shown in 1958. It's a bit scrappy, but is amiable throughout and has lots of genuinely funny scenes. Best of all it is warm-hearted, innocent and human and is utterly unpretentious. (C. M.) Pennington – Richards directs it all with breeziness and confidence and manages a great many refreshing location sequences. The cast are also engaging with Peggy Mount seen in typically wonderful form. Ever so likeable, an endearing tale with virtually no dud moments. Bright photography from Eric Cross helps too.

CAST: Peggy Mount; David Kossoff; Leslie Phillips; Glyn Owen; Yvonne Monlaur; Guest Star: Charles Hawtrey. Also: A.E. Matthews; Ronan O'Casey; Shaun O'Riordan; Alan Wheatley; Irene Handl; Willoughby Goddard; Gerald Campion; Stanley Unwin; Graham Stark; Graham Moffatt; Esme (Esma) Cannon; Frank Williams; Edwin Richfield; Barbara Mitchell; Edward Malin; Fred Robinson; Arthur Lawrence; Paddy Edwards; Alan Rolfe.

PRODUCTION COMPANY–ORIGINAL UK DISTRIBUTOR:

Film Locations – Eros Films

AVAILABLE ON DVD

FILM STUDIO: Walton Studios, Walton on Thames

LOCATIONS: 81 Cambridge Road, Walton on Thames (the Larkins' House), Surrey. The pub is "The Black Swan", Ockham, Surrey.

CIRCUIT AND APPROXIMATE RELEASE DATE:

ABC – March 1960 – Cert U – Double bill supported by "And The Same To You" (GB "B" film)

RUNNING TIME ON TV: 86 minutes

FORMAT: Black and White

NOTE: A.E. Matthews who plays the Master of Foxhounds claimed that he looked at the obituary column in The Times every day and if he wasn't in it he went to work. Alas, he died soon after this film was made.

IN THE UK AROUND THE TIME OF RELEASE

NEWS: The Grand National is broadcast for the first time on television.

POP HITS: Theme from A Summer Place - Percy Faith; Poor Me - Adam Faith

POPULAR TV: Wagon Train (US western series, ITV; The Larkins (sitcom, ITV)

POPULAR NEW CARS: Triumph Herald (1959–1971) Riley One Point Five (1957–1965)

AN INSPECTOR CALLS (1954)

RATING: **

SYNOPSIS: In 1912, a well off Northern family have dinner and celebrate the forthcoming marriage of their daughter to a young man also present. A police inspector then suddenly appears and tells them about a young woman who had died two hours earlier after drinking disinfectant. The father realises that the deceased was employed in his factory two years before and was dismissed after protesting about the low wages. The others present also recall their connection to her.

REVIEW: This is worth seeing as it puts into dramatic perspective how we can be responsible for the fate of other people almost without knowing it. The script by Desmond Davis, was based on J B Priestley's 1945 stage play and is thought provoking, although a bit dry and contrived. Guy Hamilton directs with quiet assurance and flair and is well supported by Joseph Bato's classy art direction and Ted Scaife's excellent photography. As the inspector, Alastair Sim is in top form and is quite chilling. Has a truly superb ending.

CAST: Alastair Sim; Olga Lindo; Arthur Young; Brian Worth; Eileen More; Bryan Forbes; Jane Wenham; George Woodbridge; John Welsh; Barbara Everest; Charles Saynor; Olwen Brookes; Frances Gowens. UNBILLED CAST: George Cole; Norman Bird.

PRODUCTION COMPANY–ORIGINAL UK DISTRIBUTOR:

Watergate Productions - British Lion

AVAILABLE ON DVD

FILM STUDIO: Shepperton

CIRCUIT AND APPROXIMATE RELEASE DATE:

Gaumont – April 1954 - Cert A - Supported by "Bang! You're Dead" (GB "A" film)

RUNNING TIME ON TV: 79 minutes

FORMAT: Black and White

IN THE UK AROUND THE TIME OF RELEASE

NEWS: BBC Television broadcasts the first British TV soap opera "The Grove Family", which ran until 1957. The cinema second feature "It's a Great Day", based on the series and one of the very first spin offs from a television show was released in 1956.

POP HITS: Secret Love – Doris Day; I see the Moon – The Stargazers

POPULAR NEW CARS: Austin A30 (1951–1956); Ford Consul (Mk 1) (1950–1956)

THE IRON MAIDEN (1962)

RATING: *

SYNOPSIS: The chairman of an aircraft company seeks a name for a new advanced aeroplane. He then discovers that the designer who should be with him has taken his traction engine "The Iron Maiden" to a rally. Returning for a test flight from the rally, the designer meets the head of a US airline who may offer a 100 million dollar contract for the planes. However, the American's daughter then crashes the family's Cadillac into the "Iron Maiden" and many other problems follow.

REVIEW: Whilst somewhat mechanical (!) and contrived, this is an amiable comedy and it's always good to see a British film from this time in colour. The script was by Vivian Cox and Leslie Bricusse and based on an original story by Harold Brooke and Kay Bannerman and is constructed in an ill thought out fashion, though it manages to be good natured and does have a lot of amusing incidents. Top billed Michael Craig ("By arrangement with Columbia Pictures Corporation") is better than usual here and Ann Helm makes a feisty leading lady. Gerald Thomas directs in a laid back, sometimes breezy way and expertly displays lots of alluring countryside locations. Very lightweight, but generally entertaining. Nice score by Eric Rogers.

CAST: Michael Craig; Ann Helm; Alan Hale; Jeff Donnell (a strange name for an actress!); Cecil Parker; Noel Purcell; Roland Culver; Joan Sims; John Standing; Jim Dale; Sam Kydd; Brian Oulton; Judith Furse; Richard Thorp; George Wooodbridge; Ian Wilson; Brian Rawlinson; Peter Byrne; Cyril Chamberlain; Anton Rogers; Michael Nightingale; The Duke Of Bedford; Peter Jesson; Douglas Ives; Raymond Glendenning (voice only); Tom Gill; Peter Burton; Eric Corrie; David Aylmer; Bill Cartwright; Middleton Woods; Peter Wells; Jonathan Kydd. UNBILLED CAST: Peter Byrne.

PRODUCTION COMPANY–ORIGINAL UK DISTRIBUTOR:

Nat Cohen and Stuart Levy/Peter Rogers - Anglo Amalgamated Film Distributors

FILM STUDIO: Pinewood

AVAILABLE ON DVD

LOCATIONS: Coleshill, Buckinghamshire; Woburn Abbey, Bedfordshire, Ascot, Berkshire; Henley on Thames, Oxfordshire

CIRCUIT AND APPROXIMATE RELEASE DATE:

ABC- February 1963 - Cert U

RUNNING TIME ON TV: 93 minutes

FORMAT: Eastmancolor

IN THE UK AROUND THE TIME OF RELEASE

NEWS: Until April 1963 freezing weather badly affects Britain.

POP HITS: Diamonds – Jet Harris and Tony Meehan; Please Please Me - The Beatles

POPULAR TV: Z Cars (police drama series, BBC); Steptoe and Son (sitcom, BBC)

POPULAR NEW CARS: Fiat 500 (1957–1975); Triumph Herald (1959–1970)

KES (1969)

RATING: *

SYNOPSIS: In Barnsley, Yorkshire, a 14 year old lives with his coalminer brother and separated mother. One day he takes a kestrel chick from the top of a farm building and starts to train it.

REVIEW: A decidedly bleak drama, which contrasts the idyllic countryside scenes with nightmarish school and home ones. It was based on the novel "A Kestrel For A Knave" by Barry Hines and the script was written by Hines, Ken (billed as Kenneth) Loach and Tony Garnett. It's bitter and despairing, depicting a life, which apart from the kestrel training is unremittingly grim. Loach also directed, adopting a semi-documentary approach and gets great performances from lead David Bradley, Freddie Fletcher and Bob Bowes as the nasty and terrifying headmaster. One of the best and most famous sequences is the football match featuring the hilarious Brian Glover as a quintessential 1960's games master. John Cameron's lovely score and the rural episodes offer a respite from the bitterness and pessimism. Heartbreaking ending.

CAST: David Bailey; Freddie Fletcher; Colin Welland; Lynne Perrie; Bob Bowes; Billy (Bill) Dean; Harry Markham; Duggie Brown; Bernard Atha; Trevor Hesketh.; Robert Naylor; Geoffrey Banks; Eric Bolderson; Joey Kaye. Also others.

PRODUCTION COMPANY–ORIGINAL UK DISTRIBUTOR:

Woodfall Films/Kestrel Films - United Artists

AVAILABLE ON DVD

FILM STUDIO: None

LOCATIONS: Barnsley, Yorkshire

CIRCUIT AND APPROXIMATE RELEASE DATE:

ABC - July 1970 - Cert U

RUNNING TIME ON TV: 106 minutes

FORMAT: Technicolor

NOTE: The "tag lines" on the posters included: "Both wild, both alike in their love of freedom and contemptuous of the world around them" and "They beat him, they deprived him, they ridiculed him, they broke his heart, but they couldn't break his spirit".

IN THE UK AROUND THE TIME OF RELEASE

NEWS: A docks strike leads to "A State of Emergency".

POP HITS: In The Summertime – Mungo Jerry; All Right Now – Free

POPULAR TV: News At Ten (ITV); A Family at War (drama series, ITV)

POPULAR NEW CARS: Morris 1300 (1967–1971); Humber Sceptre (Mk3) (1967–1976)

KHARTOUM (1966)

RATING: *

SYNOPSIS: In 1883, Egypt hires an army of 10,000 and a British Colonel, William Hicks, who trek 1,600 miles in an attempt to kill the religious zealot "The Madhi". However they're slaughtered in an ambush and British Liberal Prime Minister William Gladstone is subsequently pressured to seek revenge. General Charles Gordon, a man with a high reputation, reluctantly agrees to go to Egypt in order to evacuate the local people trapped in Khartoum by the Madhi and his followers.

REVIEW: A superior and different historical drama, which has stunning location sequences wonderfully photographed by Edward Scaife and Harry Waxman (Second Unit) in Technicolor and Ultra Panavision. Robert Ardrey provided an unusually literate and meaningful script, ditching the usual clichés. It's basically the portrayal of a fascinating hero and he's played in a truly superb manner by Charlton Heston. He has rarely been better and is well supported by Laurence Olivier (as the Madhi), Ralph Richardson (as Gladstone) and Richard Johnson (also in top form). One of Britain's best directors, Basil Dearden here handles things a bit stiffly, but there is solidness to his approach. The excellent score by the under-rated Frank Cordell dominates the whole film and is one of the best things here.

CAST: Charlton Heston; Laurence Olivier; Ralph Richardson; Richard Johnson; Alexander Knox; Michael Hordern; Nigel Green; Hugh Williams; Ralph Michael; Douglas Wilmer; Edward Underdown; Peter Arne; Johnny Sekka; Zia Mohyeddin; Marne Maitland; Alan Tilvern. UNBILLED CAST: Ronald Leigh Hunt; Roger Delgado; George Pastell; opening and end narration by Leo Genn.

PRODUCTION COMPANY–ORIGINAL UK DISTRIBUTOR:

Julian Blaustein Productions Inc - United Artists

AVAILABLE ON DVD

FILM STUDIO: Pinewood

LOCATIONS: Cairo and others in Egypt

CIRCUIT AND APPROXIMATE RELEASE DATE:

Odeon – September 1967 - Cert U - Supported by "Cirrhosis Of The Louvre" (short film)

RUNNING TIME ON TV: 122 minutes

FORMAT: Technicolor and Ultra Panavision. Cinerama in some cinemas

NOTE: Laurence Olivier filmed all of his scenes at Pinewood studios. Director Basil Dearden had to change his name from Basil Dear when he started in the industry as it was too close to the name of Basil Dean, a notable producer.

IN THE UK AROUND THE TIME OF RELEASE

NEWS: The Prisoner TV series starring Patrick McGoohan was first broadcast.

POP HITS: The Last Waltz - Engelbert Humperdinck; Let's Go To San Francisco - The Flowerpot Men

POPULAR TV: World In Action (documentary series, ITV); The Golden Shot (quiz series, ITV)

POPULAR NEW CARS: Ford Corsair (1964–1970); Morris Minor 1000 (1948–1971)

A KIND OF LOVING (1962)

RATING: ***

SYNOPSIS: In a Northern industrial town, a 25-ish draughtsman attends his sister's wedding. He returns to his job at an engineering company, where he becomes attracted to a typist. As their relationship develops, so do their problems.

REVIEW: Although a little over-rated, this is a superior "British New Wave" drama. It possesses a believable atmosphere and has a fascinating period feel. The script by Willis Hall and Keith Waterhouse, from the 1960 novel by Stan Barstow (1928–2011) is a bit rough and ready, but is also unusually insightful and involving. John Schlesinger, in his debut feature film, directs with real feeling for everyday life. No doubt he learned this from his previous documentary experience which included the acclaimed 1961 "Terminus", a British Transport Films short subject. There are also fine portrayals from the entire cast, with Alan Bates never better, despite his reputation he could later turn in strangely mannered performances. A good snapshot of life in Britain in the early 1960's with lots of location sequences nicely shot by Denys Coop. The art direction of Ray Simm is also notable.

CAST: Alan Bates; "Introducing June Ritchie"; Also: Thora Hird; Bert Palmer; James Bolam; Jack Smethurst; Gwen Nelson; Pat Keen; Leonard Rossiter; Patsy Rowlands; David Mahlowe; John Ronane; Fred Ferris; Peter Madden; Harry Markham; Michael Deacon; Annette Robertson; Malcolm Patton. UNBILLED CAST: Helen Fraser; Bryan Mosley; Jerry Desmonde (as a quiz show host in a television programme); Douglas Livingstone. Also others.

PRODUCTION COMPANY–ORIGINAL UK DISTRIBUTOR:

Nat Cohen and Stuart Levy/Joseph Janni/Vic Fims/Waterhall Productions – Anglo Amalgamated Film Distributors

AVAILABLE ON DVD

FILM STUDIO: Shepperton

LOCATIONS: Blackburn, Bolton, Oldham and Radcliffe, Greater Manchester; Preston, Lancashire

CIRCUIT AND APPROXIMATE RELEASE DATE:

ABC - April 1962 – Cert X

RUNNING TIME ON TV: 108 minutes

FORMAT: Black and white

IN THE UK AROUND THE TIME OF RELEASE

NEWS: James Hanratty is hanged at Bedford prison for the murder of Michael Gregsten and the rape and shooting of Gregsten's mistress Valerie Storey. Many doubted his guilt for years afterwards, but DNA testing closed the case ten years ago and indicated that he was indeed guilty.

POP HITS: Wonderful Land - The Shadows; Dream Baby - Roy Orbison

POPULAR TV: Laramie (US western series); Rawhide (US western series starring Clint Eastwood, ITV)

POPULAR NEW CARS: Wolseley Hornet (1961–1969); Triumph Herald 1200) (1961–1970)

THE LARGE ROPE ("B") (1953)

RATING: **

SYNOPSIS: A 30-ish man returns to his home village after three years in prison for assaulting a woman. He meets her again at her husband's farm and finds that she was made to lie in court. As a result he's bitterly resentful of her husband and another man who also put pressure on her to lie.

REVIEW: This is worth seeing for its fascinating depiction of English village life in the early 1950's, a very rare subject. There are a great many splendid locations which give this a wonderful atmosphere. Set against this is stilted direction from Wolf Rilla and some wooden performances. The script by Ted Willis based on a story by Julian Wintle is a bit erratic, but is intelligent and believable in its portrayal of country living. Tense, gritty and involving, one of the best "B" pictures made in Britain in the 1950's.

CAST: Susan Shaw; Donald Houston; Robert Brown; Peter Byrne; Vanda Godsell; Richard Warner; Thomas Heathcote; Leonard White; Christine Finn; Margaret Anderson. UNBILLED CAST: Esma Cannon; Katie Johnson; Edward Judd; Hilda Fenemore.

PRODUCTION COMPANY–ORIGINAL UK DISTRIBUTOR:

Insignia - United Artists

FILM STUDIO: Nettlefold Studios, Walton-On Thames

NOT AVAILABLE ON DVD

LOCATIONS: Turville, Buckinghamshire

CIRCUIT AND APPROXIMATE RELEASE DATE:

ABC - December 1953 - Cert A

RUNNING TIME ON TV: 71 minutes

FORMAT: Black and White

NOTE: The village and/or windmill have been in many films including "Chitty Chitty Bang Bang", "Went The Day Well" and "A Yank In Ermine". The village was also used for exterior shots in TV's "The Vicar of Dibley".

IN THE UK AROUND THE TIME OF RELEASE

NEWS: The BBC programme Panorama had just started its long run.

POP HITS: Answer Me – Frankie Laine; Answer Me – David Whitfield

POPULAR NEW CARS: Standard 8 (1953–1961); Vauxhall Wyvern (1951–1957)

LAST HOLIDAY (1950)

RATING: ***

SYNOPSIS: An unattached, mild mannered agricultural implement salesman is told by his doctor that he has only a few weeks left to live. He resigns from his job, withdraws all of his savings of £800 and decides to stay at an upmarket hotel. Subsequently he gets to know the housekeeper and various guests, including an inventor and a Cabinet Minister and ponders the end of his life.

REVIEW: An interesting little drama which has a bittersweet air and a double twist ending J.B. Priestley wrote the script and it is the only time he wrote anything directly for the cinema, having written many books and plays which included "An Inspector Calls". It's highly observant about human nature, has a set of believable characters and displays a rare degree of thought. It is admittedly a bit contrived and self conscious, but its qualities make up for these flaws. Giving one of his best ever screen performances, Alec Guinness is touching and vulnerable and believably portrays a man preparing to die. Henry Cass's direction matches Guinness' understated performance and he handles this with affection. Great supporting performances also help, with Kay Walsh, Bernard Lee, Sid James and Wilfrid Hyde White especially adept. An engaging contained little world is created here and Duncan Sutherland's splendid art direction is a big part of it. Nicely lit photography by Ray Elton and Francis Chagrin's sad, violin dominated score impress too.

CAST: Alec Guinness; Beatrice Campbell; Kay Walsh; Wilfrid Hyde White; Bernard Lee; Sid James; Muriel George; Helen Cherry; Brian Worth; Coco (Gregoire) Aslan; Ernest Thesiger; Esme (Esma) Cannon; Campbell Cotts; Moutrie Kelsall; Brian Oulton; Meier Tzelniker; Arthur Howard; Mme (sic) Kirkwood-Hackett; Hal Osmond; Harry Hutchinson; Eric Maturin; Jean

Colin; Lockwood West; Leslie Weston; Heather Wilde; Ronald Simpson; David McCallum (as the fiddler - the father of the NCIS and "The Man From Uncle" star with the same name). UNBILLED CAST: Peter Jones; Charles Lloyd Pack; John Charlesworth; Raymond Rollett.

PRODUCTION COMPANY–ORIGINAL UK DISTRIBUTOR:

Associated British Picture Corporation/Watergate - Associated British-Pathe

AVAILABLE ON DVD

FILM STUDIO: Welwyn, Welwyn Garden City (Sold in 1951, then used as a tobacco warehouse, now demolished and the site of a company's head office)

CIRCUIT AND APPROXIMATE RELEASE DATE:

ABC – May 1950 – Cert U

RUNNING TIME ON TV: 85 minutes

FORMAT: Black and White

IN THE UK AROUND THE TIME OF RELEASE

NEWS: The first charter package holiday from Britain was a camping one to Corsica arranged by Horizon Holidays. The company was taken over in 1974 and the new owners were subsequently declared bankrupt.

POPULAR NEW CARS: Vauxhall Velox (1948–1951); Morris Minor (1948–1971)

THE LAVENDER HILL MOB (1951)

RATING: *

SYNOPSIS: Whilst sitting in a smart café in Rio De Janeiro, a former gold bullion supervisor recalls how he managed to retire there. For twenty years he had protected gold deliveries from the foundry to the bank where he worked. Together with a new guest at the private hotel where he lives, he plots a robbery of the bullion with two other accomplices. The plan is to melt the gold down and turn it into "Eiffel Tower" paperweight souvenirs.

REVIEW: A superior Ealing comedy packed full of delightful touches. The Oscar winning script by T.E.B. Clarke amusingly subverts crime films and is full of charm. Charles Crichton directs with tongue in cheek and does a great job utilising lots of London and some Paris locations. As for the cast, Alec Guinness and Stanley Holloway underplay effectively and Sid James and Alfie Bass shine in support. One of the most likeable productions from this studio.

CAST: Alec Guinness; Stanley Holloway; John Gregson; Marjorie Fielding; Ronald Adam; Sydney Tafler; Audrey Hepburn (bit part); Clive Morton; Edie Martin; Gibb McLaughlin; Eugene Deckers; Michael Trubshawe; Cyril Chamberlain; Meredith Edwards; Moultrie Kelsall; John Salew; Patrick Barr; David Davies; Jacques Brunius; Andrea Malandrinos; Tony Quinn; Arthur Hambling; William Fox; Paul Demel; Marie Burke; Ann Heffernan; Christopher Hewett. UNBILLED CAST: Robert Shaw; Desmond Llewellyn; Fred Griffiths; Charles Lamb; Jacques Cey, Johnny Briggs; Peter Bull; Archie Duncan; Fred Griffiths; Frederick Piper; the voice of E.V.H. Emmett. Also others.

PRODUCTION COMPANY–UK DISTRIBUTOR:

The J Arthur Rank Organisation/Ealing Studios - General Film Distributors

FILM STUDIO: Ealing

AVAILABLE ON DVD

LOCATIONS: In and around London

CIRCUIT AND APPROXIMATE RELEASE DATE:

Odeon - August 1951 - Cert U – Supported by "Missing Women"

RUNNING TIME ON TV: 76 minutes

FORMAT: Black and White

IN THE UK AROUND THE TIME OF RELEASE

NEWS: A railway accident at Ford, Sussex kills 9 and injures 47.

POPULAR NEW CARS: MG Y Type (1947–1953); Ford Zodiac (Mk I) (1950–1956)

LEASE OF LIFE (1954)

RATING: **

SYNOPSIS: A mild mannered vicar lives with his wife and grown up daughter who hopes to win a scholarship to study the piano. One day he receives a letter from the local Dean asking him to preach to 300 schoolboys and their parents in a nearby cathedral. Soon after he collapses and is told by his doctor that he has only about one year left to live. This has a dramatic effect.

REVIEW: An oddly endearing Ealing drama and a decidedly under-rated entry, it's one of the best films with a religious theme ever made. Eric Ambler's script was adapted from a story by Frank Baker and based on an idea by Patrick Jenkins. It's thoughtful, understated and in its quiet way acutely observant. Charles Frend directs with care, sensitivity and subtle flair. At the film's heart is a splendid performance by Robert Donat. His sermon speech here is one of the best things he ever did on screen, it's an uplifting experience. Lots of location sequences help and give it a rural charm. Slight, but moving and absorbing.

CAST: Robert Donat; Kay Walsh; Denholm Elliott; Adrienne Corri; Walter Fitzgerald; Reginald Beckwith; Vida Hope; Cyril Raymond; Jean Anderson; Russell Waters; Richard Wattis; Beckett Bould; Mark Dignam; Lockwood West; John Salew; Richard Leech; Alan Webb; Frank Atkinson; Frederick Piper; Edie Martin; Mark Daly; Sheila Raynor; Charles Saynor; Robert Sandford.

PRODUCTION COMPANY–ORIGINAL UK DISTRIBUTOR:

The J Arthur Rank Organisation/Ealing Studios - General Film Distributors

AVAILABLE ON DVD: US import only (Region 1)

FILM STUDIO: Ealing

LOCATIONS: The village is Lund near Beverley, Yorkshire. Beverley is also briefly seen.

CIRCUIT AND APPROXIMATE RELEASE DATE:

Odeon - November 1954 - Cert U – Supported by "Hunters of the Deep"

RUNNING TIME ON TV: 90 minutes

FORMAT: Eastmancolor

NOTE: Robert Donat (1903–1958) suffered from chronic asthma for most of his short life, which may have been brought on by insecurity. It resulted in him turning down an incredible number of prestige films, including "Captain Blood" (1935) and "The Adventures of Robin Hood" (1938), both roles went to Errol Flynn and they made him a huge star. Alfred Hitchcock wanted him for Maxim de Winter in his 1940 production of "Rebecca" but Donat refused and Laurence Olivier stepped in instead. He also had to pass on "Hobson's Choice" at the last minute and of course John Mills then took the part of Willie Mossop. He once said "I never had any real security in my life until I found the false security of stardom."

IN THE UK AROUND THE TIME OF RELEASE

NEWS: The BBC radio series Hancock's Half Hour, written by Ray Galton and Alan Simpson was first broadcast. Three of its stars, Sid James, Kenneth Williams and Hattie Jacques went on to become regulars in the "Carry On" films.

POP HITS: My Son, My Son – Vera Lynn; Hold My Hand - Don Cornell

POPULAR NEW CARS: Standard Ten (1954–1960); Vauxhall Velox (1951–1957)

THE LEGEND OF HELL HOUSE (1973)

RATING: **

SYNOPSIS: A physicist who has spent twenty years studying parapsychology accepts a large fee in order to find out if "survival after death" is apparent at a large mansion "Hell House". Together with three others, he experiences paranormal activity. Amongst its disturbing history is an incident in 1929 when it was broken into and 27 dead bodies were found. Bestiality, mutilation and necrophilia were some of the things that had occurred there.

REVIEW: Possibly the best ever "haunted house" film. "The Haunting" (1963) was good, this is better. Richard Matheson's script, based on his novel "Hell House" adopts an admirably serious approach, there's no hamminess to be found here. It's also highly intelligent and has many twists and real shocks. John Hough directs with genuine flair, using lots of close ups, long shots and offbeat angles, these add to the already un-nerving atmosphere. A revelation here is Roddy Mc Dowall; he's incredibly good as the survivor of the previous (1953) investigation. Also impressing are the photographic effects of Tom Howard, Robert Jones' set design and excellent De Luxe photography by Alan Hume. The creepy music was provided by Brian Hodgson and Delia Derbyshire of Electrophon Ltd. An unusually convincing and unsettling experience with a touch of unpleasantness to make it seem even more real.

CAST: Roddy McDowall; Pamela Franklin; Clive Revill; Gayle Hunnicutt; Roland Culver; Peter Bowles.

PRODUCTION COMPANY–ORIGINAL UK DISTRIBUTOR:

Academy Pictures Corporation/Twentieth Century Fox – Fox-Rank Film Distributors

AVAILABLE ON DVD

FILM STUDIO: EMI - MGM Elstree Studios, Borehamwood

LOCATIONS: Wykehurst Place, Bolney, West Sussex. Blenheim Place, Oxfordshire

CIRCUIT AND APPROXIMATE RELEASE DATE:

Odeon - November 1973 - Cert X - Double bill supported by "Vault of Horror"

RUNNING TIME ON TV: 90 minutes

FORMAT: De Luxe colour

IN THE UK AROUND THE TIME OF RELEASE

NEWS: Princes Anne marries Captain Mark Phillips at Westminster Abbey.

POP HITS: Daydreamer and The Puppy Song – David Cassidy; Let Me In - The Osmonds

POPULAR TV: The Generation Game (BBC); Crossroads (soap opera, ITV)

POPULAR NEW CARS: Mini Clubman (1969–1982); Renault 5 (1972–1984)

LIGHT UP THE SKY (1960)

RATING: ****

SYNOPSIS: In 1960 a company director watches a village cricket match and thinks back to 1942. During the Second World War he was a lieutenant in the army. His responsibilities included a searchlight (for enemy planes) unit at the cricket ground. The five gunners and gunner - cook living in the pavilion, had numerous comic and dramatic experiences which are recalled.

REVIEW: A sadly overlooked and under-rated little comedy drama, it's splendidly entertaining, perfectly blending comedy and drama. It's funny, believable and unusually perceptive. Vernon Harris's script was based on the stage play "Touch It Light" by Robert Storey. It features rounded characters you really care about and the storyline is well constructed and involving. A great cast helps enormously, with Ian Carmichael (top billed), Tommy Steele, Benny Hill, Victor Maddern, Sydney Tafler and Johnny Briggs all in top form. Lewis Gilbert directs with considerable assurance and does an expert job with the confinement to one basic set. An endearing and involving tale with a lot of acute observation amongst the many laughs.

CAST: Ian Carmichael; Tommy Steele; Benny Hill; Victor Maddern; Sydney Tafler; Johnny Briggs; Harry Locke; Dick Emery; Cyril Smith; Sheila Hancock; Cardew Robinson; Susan Burnet; Fred Griffiths.

PRODUCTION COMPANY–ORIGINAL UK DISTRIBUTOR:

Criterion Films (not credited)/British Lion - Bryanston

AVAILABLE ON DVD

FILM STUDIO: Twickenham

CIRCUIT AND APPROXIMATE RELEASE DATE:

ABC – August 1960 – Cert A – Supported by "The Big Day" (GB "B" film)

RUNNING TIME ON TV: 85 minutes

FORMAT: Black and White

NOTE: Ian Carmichael had just had a major success with "I'm All Right Jack".

IN THE UK AROUND THE TIME OF RELEASE

NEWS: Francis Chichester had just crossed the Atlantic in 40 days in his vessel "Gypsy Moth".

POP HITS: Apache - The Shadows; Shaking All Over - Johnny Kidd and the Pirates.

POPULAR TV: Rawhide (US western series starring Clint Eastwood, ITV); No Hiding Place (crime series, ITV)

POPULAR NEW CARS: Vauxhall Victor (1957–1961); Standard Ensign (1957–1961)

THE LIQUIDATOR (1965)

RATING: **

SYNOPSIS: In Paris in 1944, a British Intelligence Major is attacked by two Gestapo officers, who are then accidently shot dead by an incompetent British Tank Corps Sergeant. Twenty one years later at a funeral, the Major meets up with the ex-Sergeant who's now a café owner. He's subsequently "employed" and given vigorous training. However he is shocked to learn from the Major that he must make sure that 40 agents, who are "security risks", meet with "fatal accidents". Too cowardly to do this, he employs a professional assassin to carry out the mission.

REVIEW: This is the best of the many spoofs of James Bond films which proliferated in the mid-1960's. It's agreeably cynical and made with lazy assurance and is always offbeat and likeable. Admittedly it is best in the first half hour and last half hour which has a surprising plot to kill The Duke of Edinburgh (!). It's a shame that Peter Yeldham's script, based on a novel by John Gardner, sags in the middle. A lot of it is silly and draggy, but director Jack Cardiff manages to rise above it all and handle it confidently. The locations including Nice are part of the high production values which give it a glossy look and there's also a superb "shooting gallery" opening title sequence by Richard Williams Films. It's accompanied by a great title song belted out by Shirley Bassey. As for the cast, the marvellous Rod Taylor is in typically amiable form and there's good support from Trevor Howard. David Tomlinson, Derek Nimmo and Eric Sykes (as the assassin!). The ending indicates that a sequel may have been intended. Very "mid-1960's", which is a big part of its charm.

CAST: Rod Taylor; Trevor Howard; Jill St John; Eric Sykes; David Tomlinson; Wilfrid Hyde White; Derek Nimmo; Akim Tamiroff; Gabriela Licudi; John Le Mesurier; Richard Wattis; Colin Gordon;

David Langton; Jennifer Jayne; Jeremy Lloyd; Scot Finch; Tony Wright; Suzy Kendall; Betty McDowall; Ronald Leigh Hunt; Jo Rowbottom; Louise Dunn; Heller Toren; Henry Cogan; Daniel Emilfork. UNBILLED CAST: Alexandra Bastedo; Francis De Wolff.

PRODUCTION COMPANY–UK DISTRIBUTOR:

MGM British Studios - MGM

FILM STUDIO: MGM British Studios. Borehamwood

AVAILABLE ON DVD: US import only (Region 1)

LOCATIONS: Edgwarebury Hotel Elstree, Hertfordshire. Nice, France

CIRCUIT AND APPROXIMATE RELEASE DATE:

ABC – September 1966 - Cert A

RUNNING TIME ON TV: 107 minutes

FORMAT: Metrocolor/Black and White (opening sequence)

IN THE UK AROUND THE TIME OF RELEASE

NEWS: Ronald "Buster" Edwards is arrested in connection with The Great Train Robbery.

POP HITS: Yellow Submarine and Eleanor Rigby – The Beatles; God Only Knows – The Beach Boys

POPULAR TV: Coronation Street (ITV); The Bruce Forsyth Show (variety, ITV)

POPULAR NEW CARS: Triumph 1300 (1965–1970); Wolseley Hornet (1961–1969)

LONDON BELONGS TO ME (1948)

RATING: **

SYNOPSIS: On Christmas Eve 1938 life continues for the residents of a Kennington, London boarding house, they include an office clerk about to retire on this day. In the other rooms, a young garage mechanic lives with his bedridden mother and on the top floor there's an elderly cloakroom attendant. The mechanic becomes attracted to the retiree's daughter and meanwhile is drawn into crimes. A lonely fake medium then takes the house's downstairs room.

REVIEW: A well made late 1940's drama, which takes a dramatic turn just before the half way mark. Sidney Gilliat's coolly confident, sometimes stylish direction and Wilkie Cooper's splendidly lit photography is enough to make this worthwhile. Gilliat also co-wrote the script, with J.B. Williams, basing it on Norman Collins' doorstep sized novel. It's an intelligent work with many twists and turns and has endless observant and human touches. There's a rare depth of perception here which makes it unusually involving. As for the cast, Richard Attenborough ("By Arrangement with the Boulting Brothers") does his frightened youth act to perfection. An atmospheric and vivid film, much better than most British productions of the time. Heavy with period atmosphere, thanks partly to Roy Oxley's excellent art direction. Good entertainment.

CAST: Richard Attenborough; Alastair Sim (hammy and odd looking); Fay Compton; Wylie Watson; Stephen Murray; Susan Shaw; Joyce Carey; Andrew Crawford; Hugh Griffith; Eleanor Summerfield; Gladys Henson; Ivy St Helier; Maurice Denham; Ivor Barnard; Cecil Trouncer; Arthur Howard; John Salew; Cyril Chamberlain; Sydney Tafler; Fabia Drake; Wensley Pithey; Russell Waters; Edward Evans; Kenneth Downey; Henry Edwards; Henry

Hewitt Basil Cunard; Manville Tarrant; Aubrey Dexter; Jack McNaughton; George Cross. UNBILLED CAST: John Boxer; John Gregson; Arthur Lowe; Ewan Roberts; opening and closing narration by Leo Genn.

PRODUCTION COMPANY–ORIGINAL UK DISTRIBUTOR:

J Arthur Rank/Frank Launder-Sidney Gilliat/Independent Producers/Individual Pictures - General Film Distributors

AVAILABLE ON DVD

FILM STUDIO: Pinewood

LOCATIONS: Burnham Beeches (car chase) and London locales

CIRCUIT AND APPROXIMATE RELEASE DATE:

Odeon – September 1948 - Cert A – Supported by "Mystery In Mexico" (US "B" film)

RUNNING TIME ON TV: 108 minutes

FORMAT: Black and White

IN THE UK AROUND THE TIME OF RELEASE

NEWS: The use of the birch for corporal punishment is about to be banned in Britain.

POPULAR NEW CARS: Vauxhall Velox (1948–1965); Austin A40 Dorset (1947–1952)

THE LONG ARM (1956)

RATING: **

SYNOPSIS: A burglar robs a safe in a London office using his own keys and when the alarm goes off and the police arrive he pretends to be the night-watchman. A Scotland Yard Superintendent and his new Detective Sergeant discover that the same make of safe is involved in this and ten previous robberies. A visit to the safe manufacturers and a robbery with tragic consequences follow.

REVIEW: This was the last film made by Ealing Studios, actually at Ealing. That was sold to the BBC for drama productions and the revised Ealing Films set up moved to MGM Borehamwood studios and MGM also distributed the remaining films. This is a superior crime drama, adopting an agreeable, matter of fact approach. The reliable Janet Green wrote the script, along with Robert Barr, basing it on a story by Barr with additional dialogue by the playwrights Dorothy and Campbell Christie. Expertly constructed and believable, it has few dull scenes and is full of engaging details. Charles Frend directs with quiet assurance and some flair and handles the numerous pleasing location sequences well. The star here, Jack Hawkins, is seen at his most likeable and turns in a first rate performance too. Lots of familiar faces such as Geoffrey Keen provide great supporting work. Fine score by Gerbrand Schurmann.

CAST: Jack Hawkins; John Stratton; Dorothy Alison; Geoffrey Keen; Ursula Howells; Newton Blick; Sydney Tafler; Ralph Truman; Maureen Delany; Richard Leech; Meredith Edwards; Jameson Clark; Ian Bannen; Alec McCowen (billed as McOwen); William Mervyn; Joss Ambler; Glyn Houston; Harry Locke; Nicholas Parsons; Michael Brooke; John Welsh; Harold Goodwin; Sam Kydd; David Davies; Barry Keegan (billed as Keagan); John Warwick; Arthur Rigby (voice dubbed by another actor); Peter Burton; Maureen Davis; Gillian Webb. UNBILLED CAST: Stratford Johns; Vincent Ball; John Paul; Fred Griffiths; Richard Davies; Frederick Treves.

PRODUCTION COMPANY–ORIGINAL UK DISTRIBUTOR:

The Rank Organisation/Ealing Studios - J Arthur Rank Film Distributors

FILM STUDIO: Ealing

AVAILABLE ON DVD

LOCATIONS: The Royal Festival Hall and others in London

CIRCUIT AND APPROXIMATE RELEASE DATE:

Gaumont - September 1956 - Cert A – Supported by "Edge Of Hell" (US "B" film)

RUNNING TIME ON TV: 92 minutes

FORMAT: Black and White

IN THE UK AROUND THE TIME OF RELEASE

NEWS: A plan to politically link Britain and France is not given the go ahead.

POP HITS: Whatever Will Be Will Be (Que Sera Sera) - Doris Day; Lay Down Your Arms – Anne Shelton

POPULAR TV: Dragnet (US crime series, ITV); Gun Law (US western series, ITV)

POPULAR NEW CARS: Volkswagen Beetle (1953–1957 model); Bond Minicar (three wheeler) (1948–1965)

THE LOVE MATCH (1955)

RATING: ***

SYNOPSIS: A goods train driver races at 60 miles per hour so that he and a fireman can get to a football match on time. After accidentally throwing a pie at the referee, he ends up in court. He borrows the money for the fine from a railway employee's holiday fund, but a woman steals it from him at the police station. He finds that when he gets home his wife has accepted the referee as their new lodger.

REVIEW: This has been dismissed, but is actually one of the funniest British films of the 1950's and also Arthur Askey's best movie. It's an amiable and breezy "Northern" comedy, which is warm, observant and agreeably silly. The script by Geoffrey Orme with additional dialogue by Glenn Melvyn was based on Melvyn's stage play. Whilst a bit episodic, it's crammed full of great one liners and amusing gags and is always wonderfully good humoured. David Paltenghi (billed as David Paltenchi) directs with lots of energy and gets a marvellous, lively performance from Askey. In support Danny Ross is hilarious and should have appeared in loads more films (the Carry On's?). A big part of the appeal here is the endearing period air, partly provided by Bernard Robinson's evocative art direction Simple minded, certainly, but ever so likeable and surprisingly and consistently amusing. Glowing photography by Arthur Grant.

CAST: Arthur Askey; "Introducing" Glenn Melvyn Also: Danny Ross; Thora Hird; Shirley Eaton; James Kenney; Edward Chapman; Guest Star; Robb Wilton. Also: Patricia Hayes; William Franklyn; Anthea Askey; Maurice Kaufmann; Peter Swanwick; Iris Vandeleur; Reginald Hearne; Leonard Williams; Dorothy Blythe; Alan Clarke. UNBILLED CAST: Russell Waters; Frank Atkinson; Vi Stevens; Sydney Bromley.

PRODUCTION COMPANY–UK DISTRIBUTOR:

Group 3/Beaconsfield - British Lion

AVAILABLE ON DVD

FILM STUDIO: Beaconsfield

LOCATIONS: Bolton, Cardiff and Charlton Football Clubs

CIRCUIT AND APPROXIMATE RELEASE DATE:

ABC - March 1955 - Cert U - Double bill supported by "Invaders From Mars" (US "B" Film)

RUNNING TIME ON TV: 82 minutes

FORMAT: Black and White

NOTE: The stage play this was based on was on in London during filming.

IN THE UK AROUND THE TIME OF RELEASE

NEWS: A train drivers strike starting at the end of March, continued into June and a state of emergency is declared by the government.

POP HITS: Give Me Your Word – Tennessee Ernie Ford; Softly, Softly – Ruby Murray

POPULAR NEW CARS: Hillman Minx (Mk VIII) (1954–1956); Morris Isis (1955–1958)

THE MAGGIE (1954)

RATING: **

SYNOPSIS: A middle aged skipper, his mate, engineer and cabin boy arrive in Glasgow in a "puffer" (small cargo boat), "The Maggie". Despite the recent refusal of a landing licence, as repairs are needed, they decide to ship an American airline manager's furniture to a remote Scottish island. Their boat then runs aground and despite the American's objection they continue on their journey. Big problems ensue.

REVIEW: This is one of the strangest British films of the 1950's and possibly the oddest Ealing comedy. It's because it's so unusual that it has a lot of charm and has an almost dream-like quality. Alexander Mackendrick directs with cool confidence and expertly uses lots of enchanting Scottish location sequences. He also provided the original story, although the script was written by William Rose. This doesn't have much substance it has to be admitted, but has an elusive, wistful atmosphere and is full of eccentric touches. Fine performances from Paul Douglas and Alex McKenzie and great photography by Gordon Dines help a lot. A very different little film. Nice accordion dominated score by John Addison.

CAST: Paul Douglas; Alex Mackenzie; James Copeland; Abe Barker; Tommy Kearins; Hubert Gregg; Geoffrey Keen; Dorothy Alison; Andrew Keir; Jameson Clark; Mark Dignam; Moultrie Kelsall; Russell Waters; Roddy McMillan; Betty Henderson; Fiona Clyne; Sheila Shand-Gibbs; Eric Woodburn; Jack Stewart; John Rae; Meg Buchanan. UNBILLED CAST: John Horsley. Also others.

PRODUCTION COMPANY–UK DISTRIBUTOR:

The J Arthur Rank Organisation/Ealing Studios - General Film Distributors

AVAILABLE ON DVD

FILM STUDIO: Ealing

CIRCUIT AND APPROXIMATE RELEASE DATE:

Odeon - March 1954 - Cert U - Supported by "Ride Clear of Diablo" (US western)

LOCATIONS: Argyll and Bute Area and Glasgow

RUNNING TIME ON TV: 87 minutes

FORMAT: Black and White

IN THE UK AROUND THE TIME OF RELEASE

NEWS: At Winchester assizes - four men including Lord Montagu of Beaulieu are found guilty of homosexual acts.

POP HITS: I See The Moon - The Stargazers; Oh Mein Papa - Eddie Calvert

POPULAR NEW CARS: Ford Zodiac (1950–1956); Vauxhall Velox (1951–1957)

A MAN FOR ALL SEASONS (1966)

RATING: *

SYNOPSIS: In 1529 the Chancellor of the Duchy of Lancaster, Sir Thomas More is summoned to a meeting with Cardinal Wolsey, the Lord Chancellor at Hampton Court. Wolsey wants to arrange for King Henry VIII to divorce the infertile Catherine of Aragon so that he can marry Ann Boleyn. After Wolsey dies, More becomes the new Chancellor and displeases the King with his support for the Roman Catholic faith.

REVIEW: An overlong, but easy to follow and quite absorbing historical drama, it has a huge reputation which is not really justified, but it provides unassuming entertainment. Robert Bolt's script based on his 1960 stage play, is deliberately paced, though surprisingly and thankfully it's not heavily theatrical. The direction by Fred Zinnemann is smooth and detached and he's ably assisted by Ted Moore's excellent Technicolor photography As More, the great Paul Scofield, recreating his theatrical role, is solid and believable and there are effective supporting performances. One of the best "costume pictures" of its time.

CAST: Paul Scofield; Robert Shaw; Susannah York; Wendy Hiller; Leo McKern; Orson Welles; Nigel Davenport; John Hurt; Corin Redgrave; Vanessa Redgrave; (non speaking cameo as Ann Boleyn); Colin Blakely; Cyril Luckham; Jack Gwillim; Thomas Heathcote; Yootha Joyce; Anthony Nicholls; John Nettleton; Martin Boddey. Also others.

PRODUCTION COMPANY–ORIGINAL UK DISTRIBUTOR:

Highland Films – Columbia

AVAILABLE ON DVD

FILM STUDIO: Shepperton

LOCATIONS: Hampton Court, Surrey; Beaulieu, Hampshire; various Oxfordshire locations including Studley Priory

CIRCUIT AND APPROXIMATE RELEASE DATE:

Odeon - March 1967 - Cert U - Roadshow, i.e. big publicity release

RUNNING TIME ON TV: 115 minutes

FORMAT: Technicolor

IN THE UK AROUND THE TIME OF RELEASE

NEWS: The Torrey Canyon oil tanker runs aground releasing many millions of gallons of crude oil off the coast of Cornwall.

POP HITS: Release Me - Engelbert Humperdinck; Penny Lane and Strawberry Fields Forever - The Beatles

POPULAR TV: Mrs Thursday (drama series, ITV); Z Cars (police drama series, BBC)

POPULAR NEW CARS: NSU Prinz 4 (1961–1973); Renault R4 (1961–1980)

MAN IN THE MOON (1960)

RATING: **

SYNOPSIS: A jolly, full time medical "guinea pig" wakes up in a field and is told that he has to leave "The Common Cold Research Centre" as he's too healthy. He's then approached by a professor and after initially rejecting an offer, undergoes 26 days of rigorous tests. However he's not aware that he's being examined for suitability to be Britain's first astronaut.

REVIEW: A bubbly comedy, it doesn't have much substance, but is upbeat and amusing throughout. The script by Michael Relph and Bryan Forbes is basically a series of comic incidents stuck together; however their work is so good natured that it doesn't matter much. Basil Dearden directs with lots of confidence and with tongue firmly in cheek and he's ably assisted by Harry Waxman's luminous photography. As for the lead Kenneth More, as ever he turns in a highly engaging performance and lights up the screen here. Lots of refreshing locations help to give it a fresh feel. This film is like a big dog that jumps up at you wanting to be loved. Very much a film of its time wherein a lot of its charm resides. Good score by Philip Green.

CAST: Kenneth More; Shirley Anne Field; Michael Hordern; Charles Gray; John Glyn-Jones; John Phillips; Norman Bird; Noel Purcell; Newton Blick; Bernard Horsfall; Ed Devereux; Richard Pearson; Jeremy Lloyd; Russell Waters; Danny Green; Bruce Boa; Lionel Gamlin. UNBILLED CAST: Dudley Foster; Edward Burnham.

PRODUCTION COMPANY–ORIGINAL UK DISTRIBUTOR:

Allied Film Makers/Excalibur Films - Rank Film Distributors

AVAILABLE ON DVD

FILM STUDIO: Pinewood

LOCATIONS: Jolly Woodman Pub near Beaconsfield, Denham Railway Station, Denham Village, all Buckinghamshire

CIRCUIT AND APPROXIMATE RELEASE DATE:

Odeon – January 1961 - Cert U – Supported by "Marriage of Convenience" (GB "B" film)

RUNNING TIME ON TV: 95 minutes

FORMAT: Black and White

IN THE UK AROUND THE TIME OF RELEASE

NEWS: The farthing coin ceases to be legal tender.

POP HITS: Poetry In Motion - Johnny Tillotson; Portrait Of My Love – Matt Munro

POPULAR TV: The Russ Conway Show (variety with the famed pianist, ITV); Sunday Night At The London Palladium (variety series, ITV)

POPULAR NEW CARS: Standard Vanguard Six (1960–1963); Singer Gazelle (III) (1959–1963)

MURDER SHE SAID (1961)

RATING: **

SYNOPSIS: During a railway journey, Jane Marple, an avid reader of detective stories, witnesses a woman being strangled through the window of a passing train. The police can find no evidence, but she and her male companion find a clue beside the railway line where the incident occurred. Believing a large house next to the line could be linked to the murder, she starts work there as a maid.

REVIEW: The first and best of the four "Miss Marple" films made between 1961 and 1965. It was also the only one actually based on a "Miss Marple" novel by Agatha Christie, "4.50 From Paddington". It was adapted by David Osborn and was scripted by David Pursall and Jack Seddon. They certainly take considerable liberties with the book, eliminating characters, introducing new ones and putting the amateur sleuth centre stage. Margaret Rutherford's typically bustling portrayal was also a long way from the author's vision. However, Rutherford is splendid as ever and the whole thing is charmingly eccentric and involving and has lots of twists and red herrings. Director George Pollock gets good performances all round and does a solid job. He's given great support from Geoffrey Faithfull's photography and Frank White's art direction. There is a theory that watching murder on the screen in these circumstances can be "cosy" because we feel safe from it all. Basically an upmarket "B" production, but more enjoyable than most "A" productions. Ron Goodwin supplies another good score.

CAST: Margaret Rutherford; Arthur Kennedy; Muriel Pavlow; James Robertson Justice; Guest Starring: Thorley Walters; Charles Tingwell Also: Conrad Phillips; Ronald Howard; Stringer Davis; Joan Hickson; Gerald Cross; Michael Golden; Ronnie Raymond (voice dubbed by another actor); Peter Butterworth; Richard Briers; Gordon Harris; Lucy Griffiths; Barbara Leake.

PRODUCTION COMPANY–ORIGINAL UK DISTRIBUTOR:

MGM British Studios - MGM

AVAILABLE ON DVD

FILM STUDIO: M.G.M. British Studios Borehamwood

LOCATIONS: Taplow, Gerrards Cross and Denham Village, all Buckinghamshire, Elstree, Hertfordshire

CIRCUIT AND APPROXIMATE RELEASE DATE:

ABC – September 1961 – Cert U

RUNNING TIME ON TV: 82 minutes

FORMAT: Black and White

NOTE: The sequels were: Murder At The Gallop, Murder Most Foul and Murder Ahoy. It was in Rutherford's contract's that her husband Stringer Davis be given roles in her films. Here he is Mr Stringer, an invented character not in the novel.

IN THE UK AROUND THE TIME OF RELEASE

NEWS: Over 1000 are arrested during a Campaign for Nuclear Disarmament rally in Trafalgar Square. CND had been formed in 1958.

POP HITS: Johnny Remember Me - John Leyton; You Don't Know - Helen Shapiro

POPULAR TV: Sunday Night At The London Palladium (variety series, ITV); Coronation Street (ITV)

POPULAR NEW CARS: Austin Seven (Mini) (1959–1961); Triumph TR4 (1961–1965)

THE NAKED TRUTH (1957)

RATING: **

SYNOPSIS: An unscrupulous and oily blackmailer visits a scientist who then shoots himself and his next victim collapses in the House of Commons. His other targets are a middle aged authoress, a young model, a pompous Lord and a popular television show host. All are requested to give him £10,000 or he will publish details of their private lives in his magazine "The Naked Truth". His victims plot their revenge against him.

REVIEW: This is worth seeing just for Peter Sellers, he's hilarious in several disguises, including TV show host "Wee Sonnie MacGregor" The rest of the cast is excellent too and it's always nice to see the likes of Terry-Thomas, Peggy Mount and Joan Sims. Even better here are Dennis Price and dear Miles Malleson. Michael Pertwee provided the script and wrote a score of very funny scenes. There's also quietly assured direction from Mario Zampi, who brings out the best in the material. One of the best British comedy films of the time, this is often delightful and clever too.

CAST: Peter Sellers; Terry-Thomas; Peggy Mount; Joan Sims; Dennis Price; Shirley Eaton; Miles Malleson; Georgina Cookson; Kenneth Griffith; David Lodge; Moultrie Kelsall; Wally Patch; Peter Noble; John Stuart; Henry Hewitt; Bill Edwards; Joan Hurley; Victor Rietty. UNBILLED CAST: Wilfrid Lawson; Michael Ripper; Ronald Adam; Marjorie Rhodes; George Benson; Edie Martin; Mario Fabrizi; Jerold Wells; Barry Keegan; Gibb McLaughlin; Kenneth Kove; Keith Smith.

PRODUCTION COMPANY–ORIGINAL UK DISTRIBUTOR:

The Rank Organisation/Mario Zampi - Rank Film Distributors

AVAILABLE ON DVD

FILM STUDIO: Walton Studios, Walton - on - Thames

CIRCUIT AND APPROXIMATE RELEASE DATE:

Odeon - January 1958 - Cert U - Supported by "Simon and Laura" – re-release

RUNNING TIME ON TV: 88 minutes

FORMAT: Black and White

IN THE UK AROUND THE TIME OF RELEASE

NEWS: Peter Thorneycroft, the Chancellor of the Exchequer, and Enoch Powell resign from Harold Macmillan's cabinet due to their opposition to increased levels of government spending.

POP HITS: Great Balls Of Fire – Jerry Lee Lewis; Jailhouse Rock – Elvis Presley

POPULAR TV: Take Your Pick (quiz show, ITV); The Army Game (sitcom, ITV)

POPULAR NEW CARS: Ford Consul (Mk II); (1956–1962); Morris Minor 1000 (1956–1971)

NO TRACE (1950) ("B")

RATING: **

SYNOPSIS: A crime novelist gives a radio broadcast for the BBC and then meets members of the press in his flat. Afterwards he is confronted by a crook with whom he was involved in a robbery years before in Philadelphia. He blackmails him into handing over £500 for a letter implicating him, but on payment of the £500 he then demands more money. After disguising himself, he murders the blackmailer and then follows the case with his police detective friend who is unaware of his guilt.

REVIEW: A superior "B" picture, it has a near "A" film quality. John Gilling's script based on a story by Robert S Baker, adapted by Carl Nystrom is neatly constructed and bright. It's also nicely offbeat and has believable characters and convincing situations. Gilling also directed and does a confident job, helping to make this surprisingly involving. As for the cast, Hugh Sinclair turns in an excellent performance and the supporting cast, notably John Laurie is good too. A tense and entertaining second feature.

CAST: Hugh Sinclair; Dinah Sheridan; John Laurie; Dora Bryan; Barry Morse; Beatrice Varley; Michael Brennan; Michael Ward; Hal Osmond; Sam Kydd; Sidney Vivian; Ernest Butcher; Anthony Pendrell.

PRODUCTION COMPANY–ORIGINAL UK DISTRIBUTOR:

Tempean – Eros Films

AVAILABLE ON DVD: Part of a box set

FILM STUDIO: Alliance Studios (Hammersmith)

LOCATIONS: Taplow railway station, Buckinghamshire

CIRCUIT AND APPROXIMATE RELEASE DATE:

ABC – September 1950 - Cert A

RUNNING TIME ON TV: 72 minutes

FORMAT: Black and White

IN THE UK AROUND THE TIME OF RELEASE

NEWS: 116 miners were trapped in a coal mine in Ayrshire, Scotland and all survived.

POPULAR NEW CARS: Standard Vanguard (Phase 1) (1947–1953); Morris Six (1948–1953)

NORTH WEST FRONTIER (1959)

RATING: ***

SYNOPSIS: In the North West province of India in 1905, just before he is killed, a Maharajah asks a British army captain to take his six year old son to the garrison town of Haserabad, then to Delhi. In Haserabad the British ambassador requests that the prince is taken to safety to a town 300 miles away. The only transport is a very old steam engine and one carriage. Other passengers include the boy's American nanny, the ambassador's wife, a French arms salesman, an anti-British journalist and an elderly diplomat. A highly perilous journey follows.

REVIEW: This does take half an hour to properly warm up, but it then becomes a splendid adventure film. The atmosphere alone makes it worthwhile, with many fascinating India set location sequences. These and the rest of the film are handled with cool confidence by director J Lee Thompson. He's ably supported by Geoffrey Unsworth's excellent Eastmancolor photography. The script by Robin Estridge was adapted from a screenplay by Frank Nugent and based on an original story by Patrick Ford and Will Price. It's surprisingly, an acutely intelligent and perceptive work and peopled with wonderfully well rounded characters. Lead Kenneth More is here seen in top form as the plucky, but easygoing and good humoured English hero. In support Herbert Lom, Wilfrid Hyde White and Eugene Deckers impress the most. A refreshingly different action picture, made with care and style and containing expertly staged action sequences. Tense, often thrilling and always involving. Mischa Spoliansky provided the winning score latterly using an instrumental version of "The Eton Boating Song".

CAST: Kenneth More; Lauren Bacall; Herbert Lom; Wilfrid Hyde White; Eugene Deckers; I.S. Johar; Ursula Jeans; Ian Hunter; Jack Gwillim; Moultrie Kelsall; Lionel Murton; Govind Raja Ross; Basil Hoskins; Ronald Cardew; Homi Bode. UNBILLED CAST: Howard Marion Crawford. Also others.

PRODUCTION COMPANY–ORIGINAL UK DISTRIBUTOR:

The Rank Organisation Film Productions/Marcel Hellman - Rank Film Distributors

AVAILABLE ON DVD

FILM STUDIO: Pinewood

LOCATIONS: Rajasthan, India, Andalucia, Spain

CIRCUIT AND APPROXIMATE RELEASE DATE:

Odeon - October 1959 - Cert U – Supported by "Honeymoon Island" (short film)

RUNNING TIME ON TV: 124 minutes

FORMAT: Eastmancolour – Cinemascope

QUOTE: Kenneth More on Henley Regatta "...when all the most sahib sahibs in England get themselves together, dress up in a lot of silly little hats and row themselves up and down a river....it was one of the things I joined the army to get away from".

IN THE UK AROUND THE TIME OF RELEASE

NEWS: Harold MacMillan wins the General Election for the Conservative party.

POP HITS: Here Comes Summer – Jerry Keller; Mack The Knife - Bobby Darin

POPULAR TV: Double Your Money (quiz show, ITV); Probation Officer (drama series, ITV)

POPULAR NEW CARS: Austin A40 (1958–1967); Ford Anglia (1959–1968)

NOW AND FOREVER (1956)

RATING: **

SYNOPSIS: In a market town, the son of a garage owner is asked to take a 17 year old girl to a school concert. Afterwards he invites her to a local dance and the next day she learns that her (divorced) father has died. Distraught at the news, she becomes close to the garage owner's son and a romance develops.

REVIEW: A surprisingly fresh and engaging drama which tackles the subject of young romance. The script by R.F. Delderfield and Michael Pertwee is certainly scrappily constructed and self conscious, but manages to be insightful and thoughtful. It's also warm and has lots of endearing moments. Mario Zampi does direct a little stiffly, but stylishly handles the amazingly extensive Cotswolds and Lake District locations. It's always great to see a British film of the 1950's in colour and this adds to the already fascinating period look. It's a glimpse at a world that's gone or perhaps one that never really existed. Leads Janette Scott and Vernon Gray sometimes struggle when the material becomes flimsy, but convey youthful innocence very well. An extremely rare film not seen on television for over 30 years.

CAST: Janette Scott; Kay Walsh; Jack Warner; Vernon Gray; Pamela Brown; Sonia Dresdel; David Kossoff; Moultrie Kelsall; Wilfrid Lawson; Guy Middleton; Marjorie Rhodes; Ronald Squire; Charles Victor; Bryan Forbes; Irene Handl; Harold Goodwin; Toke Townley (voice dubbed by another actor); Russell Waters; Michael Pertwee; Henry Hewitt; Martin Wyldeck. UNBILLED CAST: Thora Hird (Janette Scott's real life mother); Hattie Jacques; Brian Wilde; George Woodbridge; Hal Osmond; Frank Atkinson. Also others.

PRODUCTION COMPANY–ORIGINAL UK DISTRIBUTOR:

Associated British Picture Corporation - Associated British-Pathe

NOT AVAILABLE ON DVD

FILM STUDIO: Associated British Elstree Studios

LOCATIONS: Chipping Campden, Moreton - In - Marsh, both Gloucestershire; The Lake District, Cumbria

CIRCUIT AND APPROXIMATE RELEASE DATE:

ABC - April 1956 – Cert U

RUNNING TIME ON TV: 87 minutes

FORMAT: Technicolor

IN THE UK AROUND THE TIME OF RELEASE

NEWS: Premium Bonds are launched.

POP HITS: The Poor People Of Paris – Winifred Atwell; It's Almost Tomorrow – The Dreamweavers

POPULAR TV: Dragnet (US crime drama series, ITV); The Adventures Of Robin Hood (ITV)

POPULAR NEW CARS: Morris Minor 1000 (1956–1971) (no longer split screen); Ford Consul (II) (1956–1962)

NURSE ON WHEELS (1963)

RATING: **

SYNOPSIS: After passing her driving test, despite many mishaps, a young woman finds that her application to be a District Nurse has been successful. She then moves to a country village with her easily confused mother. After meeting a thirty-ish farmer on the first day of her rounds, she is called to the house of a bad tempered vicar, who lives with his unmarried daughter. She goes on to have encounters with a string of awkward patients and also two local doctors who are father and son.

REVIEW: Whilst simple minded and slightly lumpy, this is full of charm and warmth and very likeable. "Carry On" scriptwriter Norman Hudis provided lots of amusing incidents, basing his work on a novel "Nurse Is A Neighbour" by Joanna Jones. Gerald Thomas directs it all breezily and with affection, making it move along nicely. A great cast in fine form also helps with lovely Juliet Mills, splendidly dotty Esma Cannon and amiable Ronald Lewis particularly good. Lots of refreshing countryside locations, pleasing photography by Alan Hume and Eric Rogers' fine score also help. Neatly made, eager to please and wonderfully unpretentious. There are also rounded characters that you can care about. Perception is evident under the surface too.

CAST: Juliet Mills; Ronald Lewis; Joan Sims; Noel Purcell; Raymond Huntley; Esma Cannon; Jim Dale; Athene Seyler; Norman Rossington; Ronald Howard; Joan Hickson; Renee Houston; George Woodbridge; Deryck Guyler; Brian Rawlinson; David Horne; Barbara Everest; Peter Jesson. UNBILLED CAST: Lucy Griffiths.

PRODUCTION COMPANY–ORIGINAL UK DISTRIBUTOR:

Nat Cohen and Stuart Levy/Anglo Amalgamated – Warner-Pathe

AVAILABLE ON DVD

FILM STUDIO: Pinewood

LOCATIONS: Little Missenden, Buckinghamshire and surrounding area

CIRCUIT AND APPROXIMATE RELEASE DATE:

ABC – June 1963 – Cert U

RUNNING TIME ON TV: 83 minutes

FORMAT: Black and White

NOTE: Joan Sims was originally going to play the district nurse, but was re-cast as the vicar's daughter.

IN THE UK AROUND THE TIME OF RELEASE

NEWS: John Profumo, the Minister for War resigns over an affair with Christine Keeler.

POP HITS: From Me To You - The Beatles; I Like It – Gerry and The Pacemakers

POPULAR TV: Coronation Street (ITV); Emergency Ward Ten (medical drama series, ITV)

POPULAR NEW CARS: Ford Anglia (1959–1968); Austin 1100 (1962–1974)

THE OCTOBER MAN (1947)

RATING: **

SYNOPSIS: Following a bus crash which kills the young daughter of friends, an industrial chemist sustains brain injuries and attempts suicide. After convalescing, he goes to stay at a drab hotel. He's still guilt ridden and nervous with people, but a lady guest befriends him in the hotel. At a dance given by his new firm, he meets the sister of a colleague and they fall in love. Soon after the female hotel guest is found strangled on the local common and he becomes the chief suspect.

REVIEW: An engrossing closed world is presented here with atmosphere in abundance. Roy Baker directs with real flair and utilises the art direction of (Alex) Vetchinsky and Erwin Hillier's photography to maximum effect. The script by Eric Ambler, who also produced, is full of nice touches and displays intelligence and observation. However, it does not flow quite as well as it could, being a bit lumpy and it's downbeat too. Solid characterisation as well as the fine handling ensures that it provides good entertainment nonetheless. John Mills in top form and Edward Chapman (Mr Grimsdale in the Norman Wisdom films) is splendidly disturbing. Different and captivating, with a nice score by William Alwyn.

CAST: John Mills; Kay Walsh; Edward Chapman; Joyce Carey; George Benson; Frederick Piper; Patrick Holt; Felix Aylmer; Catherine Lacey; Adrianne Allen; John Boxer; Jack Melford; James Hayter; George Woodbridge; Edward Underdown; Juliet Mills (aged six); John Salew; Esme Beringer; Ann Wilton; Frank Ling; Philip Ray. UNBILLED CAST: Sid James (voice dubbed by another actor); Beckett Bould.

PRODUCTION COMPANY–ORIGINAL UK DISTRIBUTOR:

J Arthur Rank - Two Cities/General Film Distributors

FILM STUDIO: Denham

AVAILABLE ON DVD As part of a John Mills box set

CIRCUIT AND APPROXIMATE RELEASE DATE:

Gaumont - September 1947 - Cert A – Supported by "Keeper Of The Bees"

RUNNING TIME ON TV: 94 minutes

FORMAT: Black and White

NOTE: Sid James (one line and that's dubbed by someone else) can be seen as a pedestrian in the first few minutes - blink and you'll miss him!

IN THE UK AROUND THE TIME OF RELEASE

NEWS: Cambridge University allows women to study there for the first time full time.

POPULAR NEW CARS: Ford Prefect (1938–1953); Hillman Minx (Phase II) (1939–1948)

OLIVER! (1968)

RATING: ****

SYNOPSIS: Around the 1830's, Oliver Twist, a nine year old orphan, is one of numerous boys who lives in a workhouse in Dunstable. As a result of asking for more gruel, he is sold to a firm of funeral directors. Becoming more and more unhappy there, he runs away to London. Once there he meets a young pickpocket "The Artful Dodger". He is then introduced to the leader of the Dodger's gang, the devious "Fagin".

REVIEW: An incredible film, worth seeing for its look alone. It's probably the most slick and glossy British film ever, the production values stun at every turn. The Production Design of John Box, supported by Terence Marsh's Art Direction make the Shepperton studios sets look utterly amazing. Carol Reed utilises these to the limit and employs scores of stylish camera set ups and shows supreme confidence. An integral part of the appeal is Onna White's Choreography and musical sequences. Her work dazzles notably on "Consider Yourself" and "Who Will Buy?" As a whole this seems like a lot of wonderful songs with not an awful lot in between. The script by Vernon Harris "Freely Adapted" from Charles Dickens novel "Oliver Twist" is perfunctory most of the time. Lionel Bart provided the book, music and lyrics and rarely have all of the songs in a musical been so marvellous. He's ably supported by John Green, who did an exemplary job supervising, arranging and conducting the music. Also notable is the Technicolor photography of Oswald Morris. Cast-wise, Ron Moody turns in a powerful performance as Fagin and Oliver Reed is effectively sullen as Bill Sikes. Of course the grim goings on conflict with the songs and if Fagin is so rich why does he live in a hovel? It's all surface here and that is amazing. The film becomes serious and downbeat in the last third.

CAST: Ron Moody; Oliver Reed; Mark Lester; Jack Wild; Shani Wallis; Harry Secombe; Peggy Mount; Leonard Rossiter; Hugh Griffith; Joseph O'Conor; Hylda Baker; Megs Jenkins; Kenneth Cranham; Sheila White; James Hayter; Wensley Pithey; Fred Emney; Norman Mitchell; Roy Evans. Also others.

PRODUCTION COMPANY–ORIGINAL UK DISTRIBUTOR:

Romulus/Warwick - Columbia

AVAILABLE ON DVD

FILM STUDIO: Shepperton

CIRCUIT AND APPROXIMATE RELEASE DATE:

Odeon – 1968 –Cert U - Roadshow i.e. big publicity release

RUNNING TIME ON TV: 140 minutes

FORMAT: Technicolor – Panavision 70

IN THE UK AROUND THE TIME OF RELEASE

NEWS: The Post Office announces both first and second class post.

POP HITS: Those Were The Days – Mary Hopkin – (which was a number one hit for 6 weeks); Hey Jude – The Beatles

POPULAR TV: Coronation Street (ITV); Opportunity Knocks (talent show, ITV)

POPULAR NEW CARS: Morris 1100 (1962–1974); Ford Corsair (1964–1970)

ON THE BEAT (1962)

RATING: *

SYNOPSIS: An accident prone car cleaner at Scotland Yard has a vivid dream in which he's a police Superintendent. He aspires to be a policeman like his father, but is rejected when his medical exam goes disastrously wrong. However it's discovered that he bears an uncanny resemblance to an Italian hairdresser who the police are investigating for being the mastermind behind the burglaries of rich people.

REVIEW: Norman Wisdom's best film, but more engaging in the freewheeling first half. There are half a dozen superb comic set-pieces here; particularly good is the "Grand National" back gardens sequence with policemen instead of horses! The script by Jack Davies and Wisdom, with Eddie Leslie, has a surprising amount of hilarious scenes, but does goes off the boil a bit. Lively direction from Robert Asher helps and he excels himself with the extensive Windsor location sequences. In a dual role "nutty Norm" is great fun, being at his most relaxed and engaging.

CAST: Norman Wisdom; Jennifer Jayne; Raymond Huntley; David Lodge; Esma Cannon; Eric Barker; Eleanor Summerfield; Ronnie Stevens; Terence Alexander; Maurice Kaufmann; Dilys Laye; Jack Watson; Campbell Singer; Lionel Murton; Alfred Burke; George Pastell; Mario Fabrizi; Monty Landis; Peggyann Clifford; Robert Rietty; Marjie Lawrence; Jean Aubrey. UNBILLED CAST: John Blythe; Cyril Chamberlain; Julian Orchard; Tutte Lemkow; Fred Griffiths; Howard Pays; Larry Martyn.

PRODUCTION COMPANY–ORIGINAL UK DISTRIBUTOR:

The Rank Organisation Film Productions/Hugh Stewart - Rank Film Distributors

AVAILABLE ON DVD

FILM STUDIO: Pinewood

LOCATIONS: Numerous in Windsor, Berkshire

CIRCUIT AND APPROXIMATE RELEASE DATE:

Odeon - December 1962 - Cert U

RUNNING TIME ON TV: 101 minutes

FORMAT: Black and White

IN THE UK AROUND THE TIME OF RELEASE

NEWS: Freezing weather begins and lasts for several months.

POP HITS: Return To Sender - Elvis Presley; Telstar - The Tornados

POPULAR TV: Emergency Ward Ten (medical drama series, ITV); Bootsie And Snudge (sitcom spin off from The Army Game, ITV)

POPULAR NEW CARS: Austin Mini (1959–1969); Hillman Super Minx (1961–1965)

OPERATION CROSSBOW (1965)

RATING: ***

SYNOPSIS: In 1944 Prime Minister Winston Churchill gives instructions to investigate the location of the Nazis' V1 flying rocket launch site. The location is at Peenemunde on Poland's Baltic coast, where experiments are subsequently disrupted by an RAF bombing mission. It's then decided to send engineers to act as spies in a new underground factory near Hamburg. Several men are chosen, but a great deal of danger awaits them.

REVIEW: A big, splashy film which provides fine, old fashioned entertainment. It's the best of the "impossible mission" war films of the 1960's, which included "The Guns of Navarone"(1961), "The Heroes of Telemark" (1965) and "Where Eagles Dare" (1969). The script here was by Emeric Pressburger (writing under his pen name of "Richard Imrie"), Derry Quinn and Ray Rigby. It was based on an original story by Duilio Coletti and Vittoriano Petrilli. It's more intelligent than expected, generally bright, well constructed and has many tense and action packed scenes. Michael "The Dam Busters" Anderson directs with breezy assurance and some style and lets this coast along agreeably. A great cast helps too with George Peppard, Tom Courtenay, Jeremy Kemp and especially Anthony Quayle particularly impressive. Ron Goodwin's typically fine score, which has a splendid main theme and Erwin Hillier's slick Metrocolor photography add to its appeal. Topped by a well staged and exciting climax.

CAST: Sophia Loren (top billed and very effective); George Peppard; Tom Courtenay; Jeremy Kemp; Anthony Quayle; Trevor Howard; John Mills; Richard Johnson; Richard Todd; Sylvia Syms; John Fraser. Guest stars: Lilli Palmer; Paul Henreid; Helmut Dantine; Barbara Rueting; Also: Patrick Wymark (as Winston Churchill); Moray Watson; Richard Wattis; Allan Cuthbertson;

William Mervyn; Robert Brown; Karel Stepanek; Milo Sperber; George Mikell; Ferdy Mayne; Wolf Rees. UNBILLED CAST: Anton Diffring; John Alderton; Charles Lloyd Pack; Basil Dignam; Philp Madoc; Gertan Klauber; Drewe Henley; Guy Deghy; Jeremy Spenser; John G Heller.

PRODUCTION COMPANY–ORIGINAL UK DISTRIBUTOR:

MGM British Studios/Carlo Ponti - MGM

AVAILABLE ON DVD: US import only (Region 1)

FILM STUDIO: MGM British Studios Borehamwood

LOCATIONS: Holkham and Kings Lynn, Norfolk

CIRCUIT AND APPROXIMATE RELEASE DATE:

ABC – September 1965 - Cert A

RUNNING TIME ON TV: 111 minutes

FORMAT: Metrocolor

IN THE UK AROUND THE TIME OF RELEASE

NEWS: Gerry Anderson's animated puppet television series "Thunderbirds" was first broadcast, two cinema films based on it followed.

POP HITS: (I Can't Get No) Satisfaction – The Rolling Stones; I Got You Babe – Sonny and Cher

POPULAR TV: Coronation Street (ITV); Emergency Ward Ten (medical series, ITV)

POPULAR NEW CARS: MGB (1962–1980); Vauxhall Viva (HA) (1963–1966)

PARANOIAC (1963)

RATING: **

SYNOPSIS: At a church service a young woman believes that she has seen her brother, who it was assumed committed suicide eight years before. Her other brother thinks that she's going insane and meanwhile the "brother" saves her from jumping off a cliff. He then turns up at the house and proceeds to try to prove that he did not commit suicide.

REVIEW: This is the best of the "one word" title Hammer crime mysteries of the early 1960's. It's superior to the likes of "Hysteria", "Fanatic", "Maniac" and "Nightmare" - all released between 1962–1965. Freddie Francis directs with flair, assurance and is ably assisted by Arthur Grant's well lit photography. The script by Jimmy Sangster, is a mix of pleasing clichés and some intelligence and is neatly played out. Of the cast, Oliver Reed is effective as a drunken wastrel and Alexander Davion is good too. An enjoyable and well made little tale, more fun than higher budget efforts. Contains some real shocks.

CAST: Janette Scott; Oliver Reed; Alexander Davion; Maurice Denham; Sheila Burrell; Lilane Brouse; John Bonney; Harold Lang; Arnold Diamond; John Stuart. **UNBILLED CAST:** Marianne Stone; Sydney Bromley; Colin Tapley.

PRODUCTION COMPANY–ORIGINAL UK DISTRIBUTOR:

Universal Pictures/Hammer – Universal International

AVAILABLE ON DVD

FILM STUDIO: Bray

LOCATIONS: Dorset

CIRCUIT AND APPROXIMATE RELEASE DATE:

ABC - January 1964 – Cert X - Double bill supporting “Kiss Of The Vampire” (also a Hammer production).

RUNNING TIME ON TV: 80 minutes

FORMAT: Black and White

IN THE UK AROUND THE TIME OF RELEASE

NEWS: The Great Train Robbers go on trial at Aylesbury.

POP HITS: I Want To Hold Your Hand – The Beatles; Glad All Over – The Dave Clark Five

POPULAR TV: Steptoe And Son (sitcom, BBC); The Avengers (crime drama series, ITV)

POPULAR NEW CARS: Austin Gypsy (4WD) (1959–1967); Vauxhall Cresta (PB) (1962–1965)

PAYROLL (1961)

RATING: ****

SYNOPSIS: A gang of criminals check the route of a payroll van. The leader of the gang then meets the accountant at the targeted firm who informs him that the payroll contract has been switched to a company with highly secure vans. After forcing the accountant to get photostat copies of the new vehicles, the robbery goes ahead with tragic consequences.

REVIEW: A hard as nails crime drama, one of the best of its era, it's punchy, confident and full of incident. Sidney Hayers directs with real verve and injects lots of stylish touches, notably when out on location. The script by George Baxt, based on the novel by Derek Bickerton, is solidly constructed and unusually observant for this sort of subject. It's also convincing, has well developed characters and substance too. As for the cast, Michael Craig gives possibly his best screen performance, he's surprisingly good as the conscience free gang boss. Also helping is Ernest Steward's glowing photography and Reg Owen's pounding score. Tough, uncompromising and unusually cynical, it's a fine example of "bread and butter" populist cinema. Has a great period air, but it's still fresh and vivid. Distinctly under-rated, it's crammed full of tense and un-nerving incidents.

CAST: Michael Craig; Francoise Prevost; Billie Whitelaw; Tom Bell; William Lucas; Kenneth Griffith; Barry Keegan; Andrew Faulds; William Peacock; Glyn Houston; Joan Rice; Vanda Godsell; Stanley Meadows; Hugh Morton; Edward Cast; Bruce Beeby; Keith Faulkner. UNBILLED CAST: Anthony Bate; Madge Brindley. Also others.

PRODUCTION COMPANY–ORIGINAL UK DISTRIBUTOR:

Julian Wintle - Leslie Parkyn/Lynx Films - Anglo Amalgamated Film Distributors

AVAILABLE ON DVD

FILM STUDIO: Independent Artists Studios Beaconsfield

LOCATIONS: Newcastle and Gateshead, Tyne and Wear.

CIRCUIT AND APPROXIMATE RELEASE DATE:

ABC - May 1961 - Cert A – Supported by "House Of Mystery" (GB "B" film)

RUNNING TIME ON TV: 102 minutes

FORMAT: Black and White

IN THE UK AROUND THE TIME OF RELEASE

NEWS: Betting Shops are legalised.

POP HITS: Blue Moon – The Marcels; You're Driving Me Crazy –The Temperance Seven

POPULAR TV: Bootsie And Snudge (sitcom, ITV) – The Dickie Henderson Show (variety show, ITV)

POPULAR NEW CARS: Rover 80 (P4) (1959–1962); Morris Mini (Mk I) (1959–1969)

PINK STRING AND SEALING WAX (1945)

RATING: **

SYNOPSIS: In Brighton in 1880, a pharmacy owner helps to convict a woman accused of murder. At home he's very strict with his son and two daughters. The son then meets the landlady of a local pub who's having an affair, which angers her husband. A friendship develops, but the son does not realise what's on the landlady's mind.

REVIEW: A heavily atmospheric Ealing drama, which is now and then quite chilling. Robert Hamer directs with real style, supported by effectively stuffy art direction by Duncan Sutherland and Richard S Pavey's well lit photography. The screenplay was by Diana Morgan, with "Script Contribution" by Hamer and was based on a stage play by Roland Pertwee. Very good performances help from a nicely selected cast. Particularly good are Googie Withers, the tyrannical Mervyn Johns, gauche Gordon Jackson, the great Garry Marsh and John Carol. Compelling and edgy. Best to fast forward the annoying singing of which there is a lot!

CAST: Googie Withers; Mervyn Johns; Gordon Jackson; Sally Anne Howes; Garry Marsh; John Carol; Mary Merrall; Frederick Piper; Catherine Lacey; Valentine Dyall; Ronald Adam; Don Stannard; Charles Carson; Maudie Edwards; John Ruddock; Helen Goss; Pauline Letts. Also others.

PRODUCTION COMPANY–ORIGINAL UK DISTRIBUTOR:

Ealing Studios – Eagle-Lion Film Distributors

AVAILABLE ON DVD

FILM STUDIO: Ealing

CIRCUIT AND APPROXIMATE RELEASE DATE:

Gaumont - January 1946 - Cert A - Supported by "Girl On The Spot"

RUNNING TIME ON TV: 85 minutes

FORMAT: Black and White

IN THE UK AROUND THE TIME OF RELEASE

NEWS: The atomic energy research laboratory was established at Harwell, Oxfordshire.

POPULAR NEW CARS: Ford Prefect (1938–1953); Morris Eight (Series 3) (1938–1948)

QUEST FOR LOVE (1971)

RATING: **

SYNOPSIS: After a laboratory experiment goes wrong, a physicist finds himself in a parallel world, where major events such as World War Two have not happened. He also discovers that in this world he is now a highly celebrated novelist and playwright who has a decidedly rocky marriage, due to his affairs. However, he falls for his "new" wife.

REVIEW: A sadly under-rated drama which explores a fascinating and shamefully under-used idea, the time warp. Terence Feely's script, based on a story by John "The Midwich Cuckoos" Wyndham is clever and different. It's also neatly constructed and involving, somehow making what happens seem believable. There's also slick direction from Ralph Thomas. He's boosted by great production values, notably Eric (and Peter) Rogers' lovely score. As for the cast, a typically strident Tom Bell turns in a convincingly bewildered performance and Joan Collins has rarely been as good. A brave effort, although it's tempered by a certain hollowness and fails to fully exploit its' theme.

CAST: Joan Collins; Tom Bell; Denholm Elliott; Laurence Naismith; Juliet Harmer; Ray McAnally; Dudley Foster; Neil McCallum; Philip Stone; Simon Ward; John Hallam; Drewe Henley; Johnny Briggs; Harold Goodwin; Sam Kydd; Joan Benham; Howard Lang; Trudi Van Doorn; Michael Sharvell-Martin; David Weston; Alex Scott; Lyn Ashley; Geraldine Moffatt; Angus Mackay.

PRODUCTION COMPANY–ORIGINAL UK DISTRIBUTOR:

The Rank Organisation/Peter Rogers - Rank Film Distributors

AVAILABLE ON DVD

FILM STUDIO: Pinewood

LOCATIONS: Various in Windsor, Berkshire

CIRCUIT AND APPROXIMATE RELEASE DATE:

Odeon – September - 1971 - Cert A – Double bill supported by "Company Of Killers" (US "A" film)

RUNNING TIME ON TV: 104 minutes

FORMAT: Technicolor

IN THE UK AROUND THE TIME OF RELEASE

NEWS: The old penny and three pence coins cease to be legal tender.

POP HITS: I'm Still Waiting - Diana Ross; Back Street Luv – Curved Air

POPULAR TV: Public Eye (crime drama series, ITV); For The Love Of Ada (sitcom, ITV)

POPULAR CARS: Morris Marina (1971–1980) Ford Cortina (Mk III) (1970–1976)

THE RAILWAY CHILDREN (1970)

RATING: ***

SYNOPSIS: On Christmas day in 1905 a wealthy civil servant is arrested. As a result of this, his wife, son and two daughters are forced to move from their comfortable London home to a cold and rundown house in the Yorkshire countryside. The children soon discover the nearby railway line and various adventures follow.

REVIEW: A warm and good natured tale, one of the best family films of all time. Lionel Jeffries directs with laid back professionalism and makes the most of the beautiful locations. He also wrote the script, based on Edith Nesbit's novel first published in 1906 which is full of charm and humanity. Amiable playing from the entire cast helps too, with Jenny Agutter and Bernard Cribblins particularly endearing. Splendid Technicolor photography by Arthur Ibbetson and Johnny Douglas' lovely score add to the pleasure. A beguiling piece of nostalgia, made with considerable flair all round.

CAST: Dinah Sheridan; Jenny Agutter; Bernard Cribbins; Sally Thomsett; Gary Warren; William Mervyn; Iain Cuthbertson; Peter Bromilow; David Lodge; Ann Lancaster; Deddie Davis; Gordon Whiting; Christopher Witty; Paul Luty; Brenda Cowling; Erik Chitty; Sally James; Beatrix Mackey; Paddy Ward; Dominic Allen.

PRODUCTION COMPANY–UK DISTRIBUTOR:

EMI Film Productions - Anglo-EMI Film Distributors

AVAILABLE ON DVD

FILM STUDIO: EMI - MGM Elstree Studios

LOCATIONS: The Worth Valley preserved railway line; Oxenhope; Oakworth; The Parsonage, Haworth (now the Bronte Museum), all Yorkshire

CIRCUIT AND APPROXIMATE RELEASE DATE:

ABC - December 1970 - Cert U

RUNNING TIME ON TV: 104 minutes

FORMAT: Technicolor

QUOTE: William Mervyn as "Old Gentleman": "Very strange and wonderful things do happen, don't they and we live most of our lives in the hope of them".

IN THE UK AROUND THE TIME OF RELEASE

NEWS: The Beatles go their separate ways.

POP HITS: I Hear You Knocking – Dave Edmunds; Grandad – Clive Dunn

POPULAR TV: On The Buses (sitcom, ITV); Please Sir (sitcom, ITV)

POPULAR NEW CARS: Austin Maxi (1969–1981); Hillman Avenger (1970–1981)

RING OF BRIGHT WATER (1969)

RATING: **

SYNOPSIS: A 40 year old office worker becomes fascinated by an otter in a pet shop window and decides to buy him. However, it becomes apparent that his London flat is unsuitable in keeping up with the animal's needs, so they go to live in a rundown cottage on Scotland's North West coast. Whilst planning to start work on a book about otters, he makes friends with the local lady doctor. He also has numerous mishaps and adventures with the independently minded "Mij".

REVIEW: Beautiful and sometimes spectacular extensive Scottish scenery makes this a joy to watch. The script by Jack Couffer and Bill Travers was very loosely based on the million plus selling 1960 book by Gavin Maxwell (1914–1969). It takes the basic idea of a solitary writer and reconstructs the whole storyline. Warm and good natured, though fragmentary, it wins out because of an endearingly simple approach. Jack Couffer also directed and does a sensitive and un-showy job, handling the landscapes and seascapes with real feeling. As for the cast, Bill Travers and Virginia McKenna are amiable, but a bit self-conscious. Frank Cordell provided a lovely score and there's a great song sung by Val Doonican over the closing credits. Wolfgang Suschitzky's Technicolor photography also helps to make this a charming experience.

CAST: Bill Travers; Virginia McKenna; Peter Jeffrey; Jameson Clark; Roddy MacMillan; Archie Duncan; Christopher Benjamin; Tommy Godfrey; Jean Taylor-Smith; Helena Gloag. Also others.

PRODUCTION COMPANY–ORIGINAL UK DISTRIBUTOR:

Palomar Pictures International/Brightwater Film Productions – Rank Film Distributors

FILM STUDIO: None

AVAILABLE ON DVD

LOCATIONS: Seil Island; The Firth Of Lorne; Argyll, all Scotland

CIRCUIT AND APPROXIMATE RELEASE DATE:

Odeon - August 1969 - Cert U – Various supporting programmes

RUNNING TIME ON TV: 100 minutes

FORMAT: Technicolor

IN THE UK AROUND THE TIME OF RELEASE

NEWS: British Troops are sent to Northern Ireland.

POP HITS: Honky Tonk Women - The Rolling Stones; Give Peace A Chance - Plastic Ono Band

POPULAR TV: News At Ten (ITV); Coronation Street (ITV)

POPULAR CARS: Hillman Minx (1967–1970); Ford Cortina 1600E (1966–1970)

ROBBERY (1967)

RATING: *

SYNOPSIS: In London, a criminal gang steal a case full of diamonds from a car, their getaway vehicle is then chased by the police through the streets. A determined Flying Squad Inspector subsequently investigates. Meanwhile, the man who organised the robbery meets his gang at a multi storey car park at Heathrow airport. He tells them that he intends to rob the Glasgow to London mail train which will be carrying three to four million pounds.

REVIEW: It's amazing that a proper, fact based cinema film has not as yet been made about the 1963 Great Train Robbery. What happens here is virtually all fiction, which is a shame and it's a rather "by the numbers" effort, with familiar "crime gang" situations. The screenplay by Edward Boyd, Peter Yates and George Markstein was based on a treatment by Gerald Wilson; Peta Fordham is credited as a "screenplay consultant". Director Peter Yates was famously signed up to make "Bullitt" after Steve McQueen saw his car chase sequence here. He handles it in a generally detached way, but the large amounts of location shooting show real style. Contains enough twists to make it entertaining and it possesses at times an almost endearingly old fashioned approach to crime.

CAST: Stanley Baker; Joanna Pettet; James Booth; Frank Finlay; Barry Foster; William Marlowe; Clinton Greyn; George Sewell; Glyn Edwards; Patrick Jordan (billed as Jordon); Ken Farrington; Robert Russell; Martin Wyldeck; Barry Stanton; Rachel Herbert. UNBILLED CAST: Mike Pratt; John Savident; Joe Lynch; Frank Williams; Robert Powell; Ivor Dean.

PRODUCTION COMPANY–ORIGINAL UK DISTRIBUTOR:

Oakhurst Productions – Paramount

AVAILABLE ON DVD

FILM STUDIO: None

LOCATIONS: Numerous in London; RAF Graveley, Cambridgeshire; Dublin, Ireland

CIRCUIT AND APPROXIMATE RELEASE DATE:

ABC – November 1967 - Cert U

RUNNING TIME ON TV: 109 minutes

FORMAT: Eastmancolor

IN THE UK AROUND THE TIME OF RELEASE

NEWS: 40 die after a train derailment at Hither Green near Lewisham, London.

POP HITS: Baby Now That I've Found You – The Foundations; Massachusetts – The Bee Gees

POPULAR TV: Coronation Street (ITV); Take Your Pick (quiz series, ITV)

POPULAR NEW CARS: Vauxhall Viva (HB) (1966–1970); Morris Oxford (VI) (1961–1971)

ROOM AT THE TOP (1959)

RATING: ***

SYNOPSIS: In 1946 Joe Lampton, an ex-RAF prisoner of war, starts work in the internal auditing section at a northern town hall. After arranging lodgings, he goes to see a play by the local amateur dramatic society and becomes attracted to a young actress. Despite her wealthy and totally different background, he decides to pursue her and joins the drama group. Meanwhile he also becomes friends with an older actress there.

REVIEW: This has no doubt lost a lot of the impact it would have had in 1959, originally several themes including the sexual ones were very controversial. However, it still succeeds because of its engaging atmosphere, although there are a number of dull or self conscious scenes. Neil Paterson wrote the script, basing it on the 1957 novel by John Braine (1922–1986) and it's choppily constructed, but has a raw power. Laurence Harvey alone is a reason to see this; he was not highly regarded as an actor, but is superb here. His character is always believable and is oddly touching, despite (or because of?) all the chips on his shoulder. Simone Signoret also impresses and so does the marvellous Donald Wolfit. As for the direction, Jack Clayton handles it in a quietly assured, but sometimes hesitant way. Uneven, but fascinating much of the time.

CAST: Laurence Harvey; Simone Signoret; Donald Wolfit; Heather Sears; Donald Houston; Allan Cuthbertson; Hermione Baddeley; Raymond Huntley; John Westbrook; Ambrosine Phillpotts; Richard Pascoe; Beatrice Varley; Ian Hendry; Mary Peach; Paul Whitsun-Jones; Derren Nesbitt; Avril Elgar; April Olrich; Anthony Newlands; Delena Kidd; Thelma Ruby. UNBILLED CAST: Wendy Craig; Prunella Scales; Wilfrid Lawson; Miriam Karlin; Ruth Kettlewell; Julian Somers; Basil Dignam (dubbed by another actor); John Welsh; Brian Worth; Richard Caldicott; May Hallatt; Derek Benfield. Many others.

PRODUCTION COMPANY–ORIGINAL UK DISTRIBUTOR:

Romulus/Remus - Independent Film Distributors

AVAILABLE ON DVD

FILM STUDIO: Shepperton

LOCATIONS: Bradford; Halifax railway station; Bingley, all Yorkshire

CIRCUIT AND APPROXIMATE RELEASE DATE:

ABC - April 1959 – Cert X

RUNNING TIME ON TV: 112 minutes

FORMAT: Black and White

NOTE: A film sequel "Life At The Top," also starring Laurence Harvey was released in 1965. It lacks the impact of the original, but is an interesting look at the attitudes and lifestyles of the mid-1960's middle class. Jean Simmons played the role of Susan (Lampton) which was created by Heather Sears in the original film.

QUOTE: The actor Robert Stephens on Laurence Harvey; "An appalling man and even more unforgivably, an appalling actor".

IN THE UK AROUND THE TIME OF RELEASE

NEWS: United Dairies merges with Cow and Gate foods to form Unigate. Much later the company was renamed UNIQ and then taken over by Greencore.

POP HITS: Side Saddle – Russ Conway; It Doesn't Matter Anymore – Buddy Holly

POPULAR TV: The Army Game (sitcom, ITV); Wagon Train (US western series, ITV)

POPULAR NEW CARS: Austin-Healey Sprite (Mk I) (1958–1961); Vauxhall Velox (1957–1962)

SAILOR BEWARE (1956)

RATING: **

SYNOPSIS: A sailor returns home from a voyage to get married and is accompanied by a fellow sailor who will be his best man. However he finds that the relationship with his fiancée becomes strained, partly because of her domineering mother. The bridegroom, best man and the bride's father then retreat to the local pub. Meanwhile plans for the imminent wedding continue.

REVIEW: This is definitely better in the first half, after which it loses its freewheeling energy. Nevertheless there are enough funny lines and situations to see it through to the end. Things are also helped by a fascinating mid 1950's atmosphere, with Norman Arnold's art direction contributing a lot to this feel. Also to recommend it is an amazing, "in your face" performance from the unique and hilarious Peggy Mount as the (soon to be) mother in law from hell or thereabouts. In support Cyril Smith is superb as the ferret keeping, henpecked husband who fights back. The script by Philip King and Falkland L Cary was based on their 1955 hit West End stage play, also starring Peggy Mount. Whilst ragged in construction, there are dozens of laughs to be had and a highly engaging cheeky and unorthodox approach. Gordon Parry directs snappily and does a good job considering that this is basically just a collection of amusing lines. A snapshot of British life of the time and yet a delightfully unconventional one.

CAST: Peggy Mount; Cyril Smith; Shirley Eaton; Ronald Lewis; Esma Cannon; Gordon Jackson; Geoffrey Keen; Thora Hird; Joy Webster; Eliot Makeham; George Rose; Fred Griffiths; Edie Martin; Barbara Hicks; Margaret Moore. UNBILLED CAST. Alfie Bass; Michael Caine (as a sailor almost obscured at the start – just one line); Jack MacGowran; George A Cooper; Paul Eddington; Anthony Sagar.

PRODUCTION COMPANY–ORIGINAL UK DISTRIBUTOR:

Romulus/Remus - Independent Film Distributors

FILM STUDIO: Shepperton

LOCATIONS: Ealing, London

AVAILABLE ON DVD

CIRCUIT AND APPROXIMATE RELEASE DATE:

ABC – September 1956. Cert U – In the top ten UK box office hits of year.

RUNNING TIME ON TV: 77 minutes

FORMAT: Black and White

IN THE UK AROUND THE TIME OF RELEASE

NEWS: French Prime Minister Guy Mollet meets UK Prime Minister Anthony Eden and proposes a union between the two countries.

POP HITS: Whatever Will Be Will Be (Que Sera Sera) – Doris Day; Lay Down Your Arms – Anne Shelton

POPULAR TV: Dragnet (US crime series, ITV); Sunday Night At The London Palladium (variety series, ITV)

POPULAR NEW CARS: Wolseley 6/90 (1954–1959); Ford Zephyr (Mk II) (1956–1962)

SATURDAY NIGHT AND SUNDAY MORNING (1960)

RATING: *****

SYNOPSIS: A rebellious 25 year old living with his parents works at a Nottingham cycle factory. One Saturday night he goes drinking with his married girlfriend and then spends the night with her. He leaves on Sunday morning, just as her husband and young son arrive home. Soon after he meets his aunt and her son, his best mate, in a pub and becomes attracted to a young woman who is drinking there.

REVIEW: A vivid and involving drama, the best of the British "New Wave" films, which began with "Room At The Top"- also in this book. If ever a British film deserved its classic status, this is it. The script by Alan Sillitoe (1928–2010), based on his 1958 novel is acutely observant and intelligent and does not have a false note anywhere. It's directed with cool confidence by Karel Reisz, who expertly utilises lots of now long gone locations. He's ably supported by the splendid photography of Freddie Francis and Ted Marshall's evocative art direction. With its fascinating period air and sociological detail, it presents an alluring England that has disappeared. This is just part of its enormous appeal, it's also first class entertainment and deeply human and insightful too. Albert Finney's superb performance as Arthur Seaton, an angry, hard edged character is integral to its success. All of the supporting cast are excellent and another of the reasons that this is so believable. Good score by Johnny Dankworth.

CAST: Albert Finney; Shirley Anne Field; Rachel Roberts; "Introducing" Hylda Baker. Also Norman Rossington; Bryan Pringle; Elsie Wagstaffe; Frank Pettit; Cameron Hall; Colin Blakely (billed as Blakeley); Avis Bunnage; Edna Morris; Peter Madden; Robert Cawdron; Alister Williamson; Irene Richmond; Louise Dunn; Anne Blake. UNBILLED CAST: Peter Sallis; Jack Smethurst.

PRODUCTION COMPANY–ORIGINAL UK DISTRIBUTOR:

Woodfall - British Lion/Bryanston

AVAILABLE ON DVD

FILM STUDIO: Twickenham

LOCATIONS: In and around Nottingham including the former Raleigh bicycle works; the Grand Union Canal, Greenford, Middlesex

CIRCUIT AND APPROXIMATE RELEASE DATE:

ABC - January 1961 - Cert X

RUNNING TIME ON TV: 86 minutes

FORMAT: Black and White

NOTE: Albert Finney was subsequently asked to star in Lawrence of Arabia, but did not want to be tied down to a long term contract which this would have involved.

IN THE UK AROUND THE TIME OF RELEASE

NEWS: The Sunday Telegraph is launched as is The Avengers television series. The Farthing ceases to be legal tender.

POP HITS: Poetry In Motion – Johnny Tillotson; It's Now Or Never - Elvis Presley

POPULAR TV: Sunday Night At The London Palladium (variety series, ITV), Emergency Ward Ten (medical drama series, ITV)

POPULAR NEW CARS: Austin A40 (Farina) (1958–1967); Hillman Minx (Series III) (1958–1963)

SILENT DUST (1949)

RATING: **

SYNOPSIS: A wealthy and retired blind ex-businessman visits a nearly completed sports pavilion dedicated to his son who died in World War Two. At his house he's visited by a local Lord who suggests the dedication should be to all the local men who have died in the war. His son's widow later arrives and his son, not actually dead after all, then turns up. He's a deserter and further complications ensue when his wife's new husband appears.

REVIEW: A remarkably outspoken and cynical drama, all the more incredible for being released by the often stuffy Associated British set up. Admittedly this is best in the first half, but it's still worthwhile thereafter. Michael Pertwee's script was based on the stage play "The Paragon", which was written by him and his father Roland Pertwee. It takes an intriguing idea and decides not to be obvious and conventional, it constantly surprises. Lance Comfort directs with real assurance and flair and gets excellent performances from the cast. Stephen Murray, Sally Gray and the brilliant as ever Nigel Patrick all sparkle here. Different, unexpected and un-nerving.

CAST: Stephen Murray; Nigel Patrick; Sally Gray; Derek Farr; Beatrice Campbell; Seymour Hicks; Marie Lohr; Yvonne Owen; James Hayter; Irene Handl; George Woodbridge; Edgar Norfolk; Maria Var.

PRODUCTION COMPANY–ORIGINAL UK DISTRIBUTOR:

Associated British Picture Corporation/Independent Sovereign - Pathe Pictures

FILM STUDIO: Warner Bros. First National Studios, Teddington

NOT AVAILABLE ON DVD

CIRCUIT AND APPROXIMATE RELEASE DATE:

ABC – April 1949 - Cert A

RUNNING TIME ON TV: 81 minutes

FORMAT: Black and White

IN THE UK AROUND THE TIME OF RELEASE

NEWS: Longleat House is opened to the public.

POPULAR NEW CARS: Morris Six (1948–1953); Ford Pilot V8 (1947–1951)

633 SQUADRON (1964)

RATING: ****

SYNOPSIS: In 1944, a Norwegian naval lieutenant - resistance leader arrives at an RAF base in England. Training in Scotland with an RAF squadron subsequently begins for a secret mission lead by a world weary Wing Commander. Their task is to attack a mountain in Norway so that it will collapse onto a Nazi V2 rocket fuel plant.

REVIEW: This is remarkably cool and stylish and one of the best war movies of the 1960's. It's directed with flair by Walter E Grauman, who handles the action sequences with real bravado. He also treats the other scenes with assurance and sensitivity and he's helped by solid production values. There's glowing De Luxe colour photography by Edward Scaife, with additional photography by John Wilcox. Michael Stringer's production design, which involves a great pub set, impresses too. The script by James Clavell and Howard Koch captures the "live for the day" aspect of RAF life in World War Two. It's also neatly constructed and unusually intelligent, for this sort of movie. As for the cast, Cliff Robertson is in fine form as the cynical, believable hero and there's good supporting work. An integral part of the vitality here is Ron Goodwin's superb score which has a fantastic, classic status main theme. Based on the 1956 novel by Frederick E. Smith

CAST: Cliff Robertson; George Chakiris; Maria Perschy; Harry Andrews; Donald Houston; Michael Goodliffe; John Meillon; John Bonney; Angus Lennie; Suzan Farmer; Scot Finch; Johnny Briggs; Julian Sherrier; John Church; Geoffrey Frederick; Barbara Archer; Sean Kelly. UNBILLED CAST: Drewe Henley; Richard Shaw.

PRODUCTION COMPANY–ORIGINAL UK DISTRIBUTOR:

The Mirisch Corporation - Mirisch Films Limited - United Artists

AVAILABLE ON DVD

FILM STUDIO: MGM British Studios Borehamwood

LOCATIONS: Aldenham, Hertfordshire (the pub); Glencoe and Argyll and Bute, Scotland; RAF Bovingdon, Hertfordshire.

CIRCUIT AND APPROXIMATE RELEASE DATE:

Odeon - September 1964 – Cert A - Supported by "Swinging London" (short film)

RUNNING TIME ON TV: 90 minutes

FORMAT: De Luxe colour

IN THE UK AROUND THE TIME OF RELEASE

NEWS: The Daily Herald newspaper is replaced by the broadsheet "The Sun" - later to be bought out and relaunched by Rupert Murdoch in 1969 as a tabloid.

POP HITS: You Really Got Me - The Kinks; A Hard Day's Night - The Beatles

POPULAR TV: Coronation Street (ITV); No Hiding Place (crime drama series, ITV)

POPULAR NEW CARS: Austin 1100 (1963–1974); Ford Cortina (Mk 1) (1962–1966)

SKY WEST AND CROOKED (1965)

RATING: ***

SYNOPSIS: In a West Country village churchyard, a 17 year old girl, who lives with her alcoholic mother, has an altercation with the sexton. A young gypsy, who is attracted to her, intervenes to defend her and they strike up a friendship. When she was very young she was involved in an accident with a shotgun, which killed an eight year old boy and she sustained head injuries, but has no memory of the incident. Subsequently she retreats into her own world and along with her friends they bury their deceased pets in the churchyard.

REVIEW: A pleasant and endearing rural tale, better in the first half, but still consistently entertaining. It's worth seeing for the Gloucestershire locations alone, they're beautiful and glowingly photographed in Technicolor by Arthur Ibbetson. The script by Mary Hayley Bell and John Prebble is admittedly scrappily constructed and somewhat hesitant. However outweighing these faults is a sense of humour, great warmth and human observation. John Mills directs (his first and last time) with assurance, sensitivity and some style. There's also a great cast headed by an engaging Hayley Mills, with particularly fine support from Geoffrey Bayldon and Norman Bird. A sadly rare look at the countryside in a British film and a tale of innocence and a breath of fresh air. The lovely score by Malcolm Arnold is an integral part of the appeal here.

CAST: Hayley Mills; Ian McShane; Geoffrey Bayldon; Norman Bird; Laurence Naismith; Annette Crosbie; Cyril Chamberlain; Pauline Jameson; Hamilton Dyce; Judith Furse; Jacqueline Pearce; Richard Davies; Michael Nightingale; Rachel Thomas; Alan Lake; Fred Ferris; Len Jones, Talfryn Thomas; Grace Arnold; Hira Talfrey; Dafydd Havard; Anne Blake; June Ellis; Jack Bligh; Gerald Lawson; Wyn Jones; Irene Bradshaw. Also others.

PRODUCTION COMPANY–ORIGINAL UK DISTRIBUTOR:

The Rank Organisation/John Mills Productions - Rank Film Distributors

AVAILABLE ON DVD

FILM STUDIO: Pinewood

LOCATIONS: Badminton, Gloucestershire

CIRCUIT AND APPROXIMATE RELEASE DATE:

Odeon – February 1966 – Cert A

RUNNING TIME ON TV: 97 minutes

FORMAT: Technicolor_

IN THE UK AROUND THE TIME OF RELEASE

NEWS: The UK starts a trade embargo with Rhodesia.

POP HITS: These Boots Are Made For Walkin' - Nancy Sinatra; Michelle - The Overlanders

POPULAR TV: The Avengers (crime drama series, ITV); Double Your Money (quiz series, ITV)

POPULAR NEW CARS: Triumph Spitfire 4 (Mk II) (1962–1967); Renault R8 (1964–1972)

THE SMALLEST SHOW ON EARTH (1957)

RATING: *

SYNOPSIS: A 30-ish man, half way through writing a novel, learns that a great uncle has left him a cinema in his will. With his wife, he travels to a Northern town and learns from the solicitor that he has in fact inherited a run down cinema. Also there are three elderly and cantankerous staff running it in a haphazard way. Deciding not to accept a derisory offer to knock the cinema down for the use of the land as a car park for another cinema nearby, the couple attempt to make it profitable.

REVIEW: A pleasant, easy to take little film just about as near as it's possible to make an Ealing comedy without it actually been made at Ealing. William Rose and John Eldridge lay eccentricity on with a spade and adopt a bemused approach. Three of the characters they have created played by Margaret Rutherford, Peter Sellers and Bernard Miles are endearingly dotty figures. Leads Virginia McKenna and Bill Travers look on like parents watching their wayward children. Basil Dearden directs with affection, assisted by atmospheric art direction from Allan Harris and well lit photography by Douglas Slocombe. Modest, innocent and with much period charm, it has few low spots and a dozen or so very funny scenes.

CAST: Virginia McKenna; Bill Travers; Margaret Rutherford; Peter Sellers; Bernard Miles; Leslie Phillips; Francis DeWolff; Sid James; Stringer Davis; June Cunningham; George Cross; George Cormack; Michael Corcoran.

PRODUCTION COMPANY–ORIGINAL UK DISTRIBUTOR:

Frank Launder-Sidney Gilliat/Relph-Dearden/Hallmark Productions Ltd - British Lion

AVAILABLE ON DVD

FILM STUDIO: Shepperton

LOCATIONS: Hammersmith Apollo; Richmond Odeon; Kilburn, London, Uxbridge Vine Street railway station

CIRCUIT AND APPROXIMATE RELEASE DATE:

ABC - May 1957 - Cert U

RUNNING TIME ON TV: 76 minutes

FORMAT: Black and White

IN THE UK AROUND THE TIME OF RELEASE

NEWS: Petrol rationing introduced during the Suez Canal crisis is stopped.

POP HITS: Cumberland Gap – Lonnie Donegan; Rock-A Billy – Guy Mitchell

POPULAR TV: Take Your Pick (quiz series ITV); Sunday Night At The London Palladium (variety series, ITV)

POPULAR NEW CARS: Austin A40 Cambridge (1954–1958); Hillman Minx (Series 1) (1956–1967)

THAT'LL BE THE DAY (1973)

RATING: ***

SYNOPSIS: In 1959 a 16 year old lives at home with his grandfather and mother who runs a corner shop. His father left home when he was very young. He's about to sit his "A" level exams, but that morning while cycling to school he tells a friend that he's running away. He rents a room at a coastal resort and becomes a deck chair attendant and later works as a redcoat at a holiday camp.

REVIEW: A modest drama, but one with a surprising amount of charm. The budget looks restricted and the level of inspiration isn't high, but it possesses a potent blend of innocence and cynicism. Ray Connolly's script is full of observant touches that are subtle and unshowy. There is a somewhat sour tone running through it, but there's also a rooting in reality. It's directed in a neat, laid back way by Claude Whatham who manages some stylish sequences. In the leading role David Essex has a go, but is hampered by playing someone very self centred and dislikeable. The film as a whole is oddly endearing and the excellent use of songs of the time is a large part of its appeal. Generally good period detail, but what were 1970's dodgems doing in 1959? Contains a fantastic soundtrack of hits of the time.

CAST: David Essex; Ringo Starr; Rosemary Leach; James Booth (cameo); Billy Fury; Keith Moon; Robert Lindsay; Rosalind Ayres; Brenda Bruce; Deborah Watling; Daphne Oxenford; Karl Howman; Beth Morris; Kim Braden; Sue (billed as Susan) Holderness; Johnny (billed as John) Shannon; Peggy Aitchison; Erin Geraghty; James Ottaway; Verna Harvey. Also others.

PRODUCTION COMPANY–UK DISTRIBUTOR:

Goodtimes Enterprises/Anglo-EMI Film Distributors

FILM STUDIO: Lee International Studios Ltd, London

AVAILABLE ON DVD A double bill with the not so good, but often interesting sequel "Stardust" (1974)

LOCATIONS: The Isle of Wight

CIRCUIT AND APPROXIMATE RELEASE DATE:

ABC - April 1973 - Cert AA

RUNNING TIME ON TV: 86 minutes

FORMAT: Technicolor

NOTE: The title is taken from John Wayne's frequent use of the phrase from the film "The Searchers" and was later used as the title of a Buddy Holly song.

IN THE UK AROUND THE TIME OF RELEASE

NEWS: VAT is introduced.

POP HITS: Get Down – Gilbert O'Sullivan; Tie A Yellow Ribbon Round The Old Oak Tree – Dawn Featuring Tony Orlando

POPULAR TV: This Is Your Life (ITV); Love Thy Neighbour (sitcom, ITV)

POPULAR NEW CARS: Morris Marina (1971–1980); Ford Cortina (Mk III) (1970–1976)

THE 39 STEPS (1959)

RATING: ***

SYNOPSIS: A 40-ish man strolling through Regents Park talks to a child's nanny, she is then injured after being knocked down by a car. They later meet at a music hall show and then go to his flat where she reveals that she's a secret agent. She is then murdered in his flat and he escapes from her killers, taking with him a map of hers to Scotland. He aims to expose a spy ring who wants the plans for a ballistic missile. Much danger follows.

REVIEW: HERESY!!! – I think that this version of the 1915 novel by John Buchan (1875 – 1940) is far more entertaining than the 1935 Alfred Hitchcock movie! It's a ridiculously under-rated piece of populist cinema and reveals the narrow-mindedness at the heart of film criticism. Worth seeing for Kenneth More alone and here seen at the height of his stardom, he's excellent as Richard Hannay. Frank Harvey's script twists and turns admirably and is full of both good humour and real tension. It's directed with lots of style by Ralph Thomas, this is quite his most accomplished work. The wonderful and extensive location sequences in Scotland are handled with particular flair. An overlooked, fast paced little gem. Engaging Eastmancolor photography by Ernest Steward.

CAST: Kenneth More; Taina Elg; Brenda De Banzie; Barry Jones; Reginald Beckwith; Faith Brook; Michael Goodliffe; James Hayter; Duncan Lamont; Sid James; Jameson Clark; Andrew Cruickshank; Leslie Dwyer; Joan Hickson; Brian Oulton; Betty Henderson. UNBILLED CAST: Harry Towb; Sam Kydd; Michael Brennan; William Mervyn; Marianne Stone; Hal Osmond; Anthony Sagar; Victor Brooks; Davy Kaye; Howard Lang.

PRODUCTION COMPANY–UK DISTRIBUTOR:

The Rank Organisation Film Productions/Betty E Box - Rank Film Distributors

AVAILABLE ON DVD

FILM STUDIO: Pinewood

LOCATIONS: The Trossachs area of Scotland

CIRCUIT AND APPROXIMATE RELEASE DATE:

Odeon - March 1959 - Cert U – Supported by "No Room For Wild Animals" (documentary)

RUNNING TIME ON TV: 89 minutes

FORMAT: Eastmancolor

NOTE: Kenneth More had been a big star since "Reach For The Sky" in 1956, but his film career faded around 1962. He blamed getting drunk at a film industry dinner and insulting the then head of the Rank Organisation. As a result he was not given leave from his Rank contract to play the role that David Niven eventually took in "The Guns of Navarone". It could be argued that the kind of role he played was falling out of favour anyway and that his cinema career would have inevitably declined. Around 1962 Ian Carmichael, a top film comedy star, found roles in the cinema began to dry up too. Their careers as top British movie stars ran almost parallel. However, in 1967 More revived his career as Jolyon in BBC TV's enormously popular "The Forsyte Saga".

IN THE UK AROUND THE TIME OF RELEASE

NEWS: School leaving age was raised to 15.

POP HITS: Side Saddle - Russ Conway; Smoke Gets In Your Eyes - The Platters

POPULAR TV: The Army Game (sitcom, ITV); Wagon Train (US western series, ITV)

POPULAR NEW CARS: MG Roadster/Coupe (1955–1962); Ford Popular (100E) (1959–1962)

THIS HAPPY BREED (1944)

RATING: ***

SYNOPSIS: In 1919, at the end of the Great War, an ex-soldier and members of his family move into a house in Clapham, South London. He discovers that his next door neighbour is an old army friend and they renew their friendship. With his wife and neighbour he attends a victory parade and then begins work at a travel agent. A visit to the British Empire Exhibition at Wembley in 1924 follows and various events and experiences ensue in the next fifteen years.

REVIEW: A surprisingly touching and believable family drama, one of the very best British films of the 1940's. It's worth seeing for its' look alone, there is wonderful and then very rare use of Technicolor, here expertly used by cinematographer Ronald Neame. There's also great work from G.E. Calthrop "Art Supervisor to Noel Coward" and C. P. Norman, the art director. Whilst there aren't that many sets as most of this is staged in one house, it's all fascinatingly evocative. David Lean directs his first solo film with both flair and affection. He's also listed on the script credit, followed by Ronald Neame, and Anthony Havelock-Allan. Based on Noel Coward's stage play, it's an unusually intelligent and human effort, still streets ahead of modern television soap operas. They make you care about the characters and the cast is seen in top form. Here Robert Newton is a revelation, this is probably his best screen performance, the expected hamminess (though it was always fun) is not here at all. In support John Mills and Kay Walsh are both convincing and charming too. Perceptive, stylish and now and then highly emotional.

CAST: Robert Newton; Celia Johnson; John Mills; Kay Walsh; Stanley Holloway; Alison Leggatt; Amy Veness; John Blythe; Guy Verney; Eileen Erskine; Merle Tottenham; Betty Fleetwood. UNBILLED CAST: Opening narration by Laurence Olivier.

PRODUCTION COMPANY–ORIGINAL UK DISTRIBUTOR:

Two Cities/Cineguild - Eagle-Lion Film Distributors

AVAILABLE ON DVD

FILM STUDIO: Denham

CIRCUIT AND APPROXIMATE RELEASE DATE:

Gaumont - August 1944 - Cert A - The biggest hit at the British cinema box office hit in 1944.

RUNNING TIME ON TV: 106 minutes

FORMAT: Technicolor

IN THE UK AROUND THE TIME OF RELEASE

NEWS: The Eleven Plus exam was introduced to stream students into secondary modern or Grammar schools.

POPULAR NEW CARS: Morris Eight (1935–1948); Austin Twelve (1939–1947)

THREE MEN IN A BOAT (1956)

RATING: **

SYNOPSIS: Set in around 1910, a 40-ish confirmed bachelor is being pressurised into marriage, so decides to escape the situation and take a vacation. Together with two friends, they visit Hampton Court maze and afterwards decide to go on a boating holiday on the River Thames.

REVIEW: The famous 1889 novel by Jerome K Jerome (1859–1927) is here turned into a broad, decidedly unsubtle farce which will have purists screaming in pain. It's frantic, high energy stuff, but worth seeing for the splendid River Thames locations, of which there are an incredible amount. These are glowingly photographed in Eastman Colour by Eric Cross (billed as "Lighting Cameraman"). The credits state that it's "freely adapted" with the "adaptation, additional scenes and screenplay" by Hubert Gregg and Vernon Harris. It concentrates on slapstick and awkward romantic encounters and seems over eager to provide laughs. Ken Annakin directs it all with over the top enthusiasm as if to try to cover up the cartoon strip goings on. It might have worked better if it had been slower and more lyrical. Despite the "sledgehammer to crack a nut" approach it's likeable and entertaining nonetheless. How? I don't know!

CAST: David Tomlinson (best player);Laurence Harvey; Jimmy Edwards; Shirley Eaton; Jill Ireland; Lisa Gastoni; Martita Hunt; Noelle Middleton; Robertson Hare; Adrienne Corri; Miles Malleson; A.E. Matthews; Ernest Thesiger; Campbell Cotts; Harold Goodwin; Norman Rossington; Esma Cannon; Joan Haythorne; Charles Lloyd Pack; George Woodbridge; Toke Townley; Hal Osmond; Christian Duvaleix; Stuart Saunders; Shane Cordell. Also others.

PRODUCTION COMPANY–UK DISTRIBUTOR:

Romulus/Remus - Independent Film Distributors

AVAILABLE ON DVD

FILM STUDIO: Shepperton

LOCATIONS: River Thames locations including The Angel On The Bridge pub, Henley on Thames; Hambleden Mill; Boulters Lock, Maidenhead and Hampton Court.

CIRCUIT AND APPROXIMATE RELEASE DATE:

ABC - January 1957- Cert U

RUNNING TIME ON TV: 86 minutes

FORMAT: Eastman Colour

IN THE UK AROUND THE TIME OF RELEASE

NEWS: Prime Minister Anthony Eden resigns due to ill health, and is succeeded by Harold Macmillan.

POP HITS: Singing The Blues – Tommy Steele And The Steelmen; Singing The Blues – Guy Mitchell

POPULAR TV: Boyd QC (legal drama series, ITV); Double Your Money (quiz series, ITV)

POPULAR NEW CARS: Ford Consul (Mk II) (1956–1962); Standard Vanguard (III) (1955–1958)

THE TITFIELD THUNDERBOLT (1953)

RATING: ***

SYNOPSIS: In May 1952, a closure notice affecting a rural branch line is put up at a local station. The local squire and solicitor visit a vicar to discuss the matter. They propose to buy the line from British Railways, with the money provided by a heavy drinking resident, who has been promised a bar on board the train. A Ministry of Transport enquiry results in them being given one month to prove the viability. However a local coach company connive to ruin their plans.

REVIEW: An absolute delight, a strangely under-rated film and it may be cinematic blasphemy, but I believe it's the best Ealing comedy. It's worth seeing for the superb extensive location sequences alone. Douglas Slocombe's glowing Technicolour photography adds immeasurably to the look. The whole thing is a beguiling glimpse of a bygone England or probably one that never existed. Whilst slightly silly and over the top at times, the script by T.E.B. Clarke is warm, quirky and quintessentially English. It's directed with laid back assurance and often stylishly by Charles Crichton who captures a fascinating time splendidly. The characters are endearing too and the performances are charming and lively. Affectionate, wonderfully different and with a hypnotic period air. Lovely score by Georges Auric.

CAST: Stanley Holloway; John Gregson; George Relph; Naunton Wayne; Godfrey Tearle; Hugh Griffith; Sid James; Jack MacGowran; Ewan Roberts; Reginald Beckwith; Gabrielle Brune; Edie Martin; Michael Trubshawe; Herbert C Walton; Campbell Singer; Frank Atkinson; Wensley Pithey; John Rudling; Nancy O'Neil; Harold Alford; Ted Burbidge; Frank Green. UNBILLED CAST: Hilda Fenemore.

PRODUCTION COMPANY–ORIGINAL UK DISTRIBUTOR:

The J Arthur Rank Organisation/Ealing Studios - General Film Distributors

AVAILABLE ON DVD Including a special 60th anniversary edition with additional featurettes

FILM STUDIO: Ealing

LOCATIONS: Freshford (the village); Monkton Combe (the station), and other Somerset locations; Woodstock, Oxfordshire

CIRCUIT AND APPROXIMATE RELEASE DATE:

Odeon - April 1953 - Cert U – Supported by "San Antone" (US "A" western)

RUNNING TIME ON TV: 80 minutes

FORMAT: Technicolor

IN THE UK AROUND THE TIME OF RELEASE

NEWS: Queen Mary dies; the Christie murder victims are discovered at 10 Rillington Place in London.

POP HITS: I Believe - Frankie Laine; How Much Is That Doggie In The Window - Lita Roza

POPULAR NEW CARS: Morris Minor (Series 2) (1952–1956); Ford Zodiac (Mk I) (1950–1956)

TOUCH AND GO (1955)

RATING: **

SYNOPSIS: A 40 year old designer at a furniture company becomes angry at resistance to his advanced designs. He tells his family that he wants them to emigrate to Australia and then resigns. Their house is put on the market, but his daughter meets an engineering student which may affect their plans.

REVIEW: This is worth seeing for its amazing mid 1950's period feel alone. Douglas Slocombe's rich Technicolor photography and the evocative art direction of Edward Carrick make it fascinating to look at. As a whole it's certainly lightweight, but is full of good humour and is actually very funny now and then. A revelation here is Jack Hawkins's excellent comic performance, his moments of exasperation are particularly amusing. William Rose's script was based on an original story by him and Tania Rose and is full of affection and acute observation, as well as laughs. Michael Truman directs it all in a warm, tongue in cheek manner and also injects a fair amount of style. An overlooked little film.

CAST: Jack Hawkins; Margaret Johnston; Roland Culver; John Fraser; June Thorburn; James Hayter; Alison Leggatt; Margaret Halstan; Henry Longhurst; Basil Dignam; Bessie Love; Gabrielle Brune; Elizabeth Winch (Liz Fraser); Alfred Burke; Margaret Courtenay; Arthur Howard; Jacques Cey; Warwick Ashton; Dorothy White; Eric Phillips; Michael Corcoran; John Carroll; Peter Hunt. UNBILLED CAST: Heather Sears; Lockwood West.

PRODUCTION COMPANY–UK DISTRIBUTOR:

The J Arthur Rank Organisation/Ealing Studios - J Arthur Rank Film Distributors

AVAILABLE ON DVD

FILM STUDIO: Ealing

CIRCUIT AND APPROXIMATE RELEASE DATE:

Gaumont - November – 1955 - Cert U – Support by "Armand and Michaela Denis Among The Headhunters" (documentary)

RUNNING TIME ON TV: 81 minutes

FORMAT: Technicolor

IN THE UK AROUND THE TIME OF RELEASE

NEWS: A derailment on the railway line near Didcot, Berkshire kills 11 people and injures 163.

POP HITS: Rock Around The Clock - Bill Haley And His Comets; Hernando's Hideaway – The Johnston Brothers

POPULAR TV: I Love Lucy (US comedy series, ITV); Sunday Night At The London Palladium (variety series, ITV)

POPULAR NEW CARS: Standard Ten (1953–1961); Austin A30 (1951–1956)

TOWN ON TRIAL (1957)

RATING: **

SYNOPSIS: A handcuffed, unidentified man is brought to a police station after confessing to a murder, and a police superintendent then recalls events leading to his arrest. A woman is found murdered and the police officer investigates a number of local people, some at a local country club where her body was found. There are several suspects.

REVIEW: This has a heavy and fascinating mid - 1950's period atmosphere to recommend it. There's also stylish direction from John Guillermin who expertly uses lots of location sequences. John Elphick's evocative art direction assists him every step of the way. The script by Robert Westerby and Ken Hughes manages to blend sleaze and corn with unusual intelligence and observation, although it's a bit thrown together. At the heart of this film there's a typically first rate performance from John Mills, he's in superb form here. Derek Farr and Alec McCowen provide solid supporting portrayals. Full of wonderful touches, involving humour, depth and chills.

CAST: John Mills; Charles Coburn; Derek Farr; Alec McCowen; Barbara Bates; Fay Compton; Geoffrey Keen; Margaretta Scott; Meredith Edwards; Harry Locke; Raymond Huntley; Harry Fowler; Maureen Connell; Newton Blick; Oscar Quitak; Trottie (Totti) Truman-Taylor; Grace Arnold; Magda Miller and "Introducing Elizabeth Seal as Fiona". UNBILLED CAST: Dandy Nichols; John Warwick; Hal Osmond.

PRODUCTION COMPANY–UK DISTRIBUTOR:

Maxwell Setton/Marksman Films - Columbia

AVAILABLE ON DVD: US import only (Region 1)

FILM STUDIO: Shepperton

LOCATIONS: Weybridge, Surrey

CIRCUIT AND APPROXIMATE RELEASE DATE:

Gaumont – February 1957 - Cert A – Supported by "Reprisal" (US "B" film)

RUNNING TIME ON TV: 92 minutes

FORMAT: Black and White

NOTE: John Mills had the longest and most consistent starring career in the British film industry, appearing in top billed roles from the mid 1940's for over 40 years. His general image is a false one: stiff upper lip military figures. Yes, he did play many of these roles, but look at him as a determined detective here, as the bemused outsider in "The History of Mr Polly" or as the haunted and unhappy figure in "The October Man". A consummate British film star and a very rare instance of one who did not further his career in Hollywood where he was offered contracts, but turned them down. He was an exceptionally gifted actor and by all accounts a thoroughly nice man to boot, not a common combination.

IN THE UK AROUND THE TIME OF RELEASE

NEWS: Broadcasting between 6pm and 7 pm began on BBC television. Previously there were no broadcasts so that parents could put their children to bed.

POP HITS: The Garden Of Eden – Frankie Vaughan; Young Love - Tab Hunter

POPULAR TV: Sunday Night At The London Palladium (variety series, ITV); Armchair Theatre (drama series, ITV)

POPULAR NEW CARS: Singer Gazelle (1956–1958); Fiat 500 (1957–1975)

TREAD SOFTLY STRANGER (1958)

RATING: **

SYNOPSIS: After a threatening phone call from his bookmaker, a gambler leaves his flat and travels to the northern town that he lived in as a child. He visits a working men's club and then rents a room next to where his brother lives. Soon after he learns that his brother, a clerk, has stolen £300 from his firm's payroll. He has eight days to put it back before an auditor runs a check.

REVIEW: Although rather downbeat to say the least, this is a decidedly under-rated crime drama. Elven Webb's seedy art direction means that it has a fascinating look and conjures up its period brilliantly. The script by George Minter (the Managing Director of Renown Pictures) and Denis O'Dell, was based on the 1953 stage play "Blind Alley" (uncredited) by Jack Popplewell. Whilst it's grim, it does possess intelligence and wisdom. Gordon Parry directs with style and confidence and handles the location sequences nicely. It also helps that all three of the stars, Diana Dors, George Baker and Terence Morgan are seen in top form. Overloaded with paranoia, it's compelling stuff that plays like a seriously upmarket "B" picture. Has a wonderful ending.

CAST: Diana Dors; George Baker; Terence Morgan; Patrick Allen; Jane Griffiths; Joseph Tomelty; Maureen Delany; Thomas Heathcote; Russell Napier; Andrew Keir; Timothy Bateson; John Salew; Michael Golden; George Merritt; Hal Osmond; Norman Pierce; Norman Macowan; Betty Warren; Jack McNaughton; Chris Fay; Terry Baker; Patrick Crean; Sandra Francis. UNBILLED CAST: Wilfrid Lawson; Jerold Wells.

PRODUCTION COMPANY–UK DISTRIBUTOR:

George Minter/Alderdale - Renown

AVAILABLE ON DVD

FILM STUDIO: Walton Studios

LOCATIONS: Rotherham

CIRCUIT AND APPROXIMATE RELEASE DATE:

Gaumont - August 1958 - Cert A - Double bill supported by "The Bride Is Too Beautiful" (Brigitte Bardot)

RUNNING TIME ON TV: 79 minutes

FORMAT: Black and White

IN THE UK AROUND THE TIME OF RELEASE

NEWS: Debutantes ceased being presented at court.

POP HITS: When – The Kalin Twins; All I Have To Do Is Dream and Claudette –The Everly Brothers

POPULAR TV: Wagon Train (US western series, ITV); Emergency Ward Ten (medical drama series, ITV)

POPULAR NEW CARS: Morris Oxford (1954–1971); Rover 74 (1954–1959)

TWO WAY STRETCH (1960)

RATING: ***

SYNOPSIS: Three convicts enjoy an easy life at a prison. The governor is meanwhile visited by a crook disguised as a vicar who then discusses a jewel robbery with one of the prisoners. Their plan is to escape, carry out the raid and return to their cell giving them the perfect alibi. However, a particularly stern new prison officer might upset their plans.

REVIEW: One of the very best British comedies of the early 1960's. It's worth seeing for the cast alone, notably Lionel Jeffries, this is probably his best film appearance - he's hilarious. The script by John Warren and Len Heath, with additional dialogue by Alan Hackney is a bit episodic but is always amiable. It also has a couple of dozen wonderfully funny sequences and a pleasing irreverent, cynical tone. Robert Day directs with quiet assurance and tongue firmly in cheek and handles the many locations expertly. Still fresh and lively and it's splendidly British and solidly entertaining.

CAST: Peter Sellers (strangely subdued); Lionel Jeffries; Wilfrid Hyde White; Bernard Cribbins; David Lodge; Maurice Denham; Liz Fraser; Irene Handl; Thorley Walters; Beryl Reid; George Woodbridge; Warren Mitchell; Cyril Chamberlain; Walter Hudd; John Glyn Jones; Arthur Mullard; Mario Fabrizi; John Wood; John Harvey; Ian Wilson; John Vivyan (Johnny Vyvyan); Joe Gibbons; Noel Hood; Myrette Morven; Wallas Eaton. Also others. UNBILLED CAST: Larry (Laurence) Taylor.

PRODUCTION COMPANY–ORIGINAL UK DISTRIBUTOR:

British Lion Films/Tudor Productions/John Harvel Productions/ George and Alfred Black/Shepperton Productions - British Lion

AVAILABLE ON DVD

FILM STUDIO: Shepperton

LOCATIONS: Willems Barracks, Aldershot, Hampshire; Windsor and Eton Central railway station, Windsor, Berkshire

CIRCUIT AND APPROXIMATE RELEASE DATE:

ABC - February 1960 - Cert U

RUNNING TIME ON TV: 84 minutes

FORMAT: Black and White

NOTE: Wilfrid Hyde White (1903–1991) was born in Bourton-on-the-Water, the tourist hotspot in the Cotswolds and is buried there. He was mainly based in Hollywood from 1963 onwards, but appeared in the BBC radio series "The Men from the Ministry", from 1962–1965 and lived in a film industry retirement home in the last years of his life. Quote from him: "I've owned 12 horses, 7 Rolls Royce's and I've had mistresses in Paris, London and New York and none of it made me happy".

IN THE UK AROUND THE TIME OF RELEASE

NEWS: Prince Andrew, The Duke of York is born.

POP HITS: Why - Anthony Newley; Poor Me - Adam Faith

POPULAR TV: Sunday Night At The London Palladium (variety series, ITV); Wagon Train (US western series, ITV)

POPULAR NEW CARS: Renault Dauphine (1956–1967); Fiat 500 (1957–1975)

VICTIM (1961)

RATING: **

SYNOPSIS: A young labourer runs away from a building site when he sees a police car arrive. He phones a friend for help and also a barrister who becomes very angry. After meeting other friends, he's arrested in a café for stealing money from his employers. His link to the barrister then becomes apparent.

REVIEW: It's now difficult to imagine the impact this must have had when originally released in 1961. It tackles a then taboo subject and was the first film in English to use the word "homosexual". Dirk Bogarde risked his career here playing a married man who's attracted to men, he's stunningly good and turns in his best ever performance. In support there's excellent support from John Barrie, Norman Bird and especially Charles Lloyd Pack and Derren Nesbitt is outstanding as the frightening blackmailer. The script by Janet Green and John McCormick plays out like a cross between jigsaw puzzle and nightmare and is as disturbing as many chiller films. Basil Dearden directs in a slick manner with excellent support from Otto Heller's wonderfully lit photography. Philip Green's score is also an integral part of its appeal. In its way sensationalist, but also sincere, intelligent and a powerful attack on homophobia.

CAST: Dirk Bogarde; Sylvia Syms; Dennis Price; John Barrie; Charles Lloyd Pack; Norman Bird; Derren Nesbitt; Anthony Nicholls; Peter Copley; Peter McEnery; Donald Churchill; John Cairney; Nigel Stock; Frank Petit; Hilton Edwards; Noel Howlett; Alan Howard; Mavis Villiers; Alan MacNaughton. UNBILLED CAST: Victor Brooks; John Bennett; Frank Thornton; Basil Dignam; John Boxer.

PRODUCTION COMPANY–UK DISTRIBUTOR:

The Rank Organisation/Allied Film Makers/Parkway - Rank Film Distributors

AVAILABLE ON DVD

FILM STUDIO: Pinewood

LOCATIONS: Various in London including Covent Garden, Charing Cross Road and Chiswick; Uxbridge: High Street (Regal Cinema), Vine Street (Randalls department store)

CIRCUIT AND APPROXIMATE RELEASE DATE:

Odeon – September 1961 - Cert X – Supported by "Attempt To Kill" (GB "B" film)

RUNNING TIME ON TV: 96 minutes

FORMAT: Black and White

IN THE UK AROUND THE TIME OF RELEASE

NEWS: The first Mothercare shop is opened.

POP HITS: Well I Ask You – Eden Kane; Halfway To Paradise – Billy Fury

POPULAR TV: Harpers West One (drama series, ITV); Sunday Night At The London Palladium (variety series, ITV)

POPULAR NEW CARS: Heinkel (200) (a "bubble car") (1956–1961); Wolseley 1500 (1957–1965)

VILLAGE OF THE DAMNED (1960)

RATING: **

SYNOPSIS: Just before eleven one morning all of the inhabitants of a village suddenly fall unconscious. When the villagers regain composure, a local scientist and his brother in law, an army major, investigate. The scientist's wife and all of the other local women of child bearing age discover that they are pregnant and give birth on the same day. The children seem to be super-human.

REVIEW: An engaging blend of village life and offbeat chills, helped by a number of highly appealing locations. The script by Stirling Silliphant, Wolf Rilla and George Barclay was based on the 1957 novel "The Midwich Cuckoos" by John Wyndham (1903–1969). It's neatly constructed and intelligent and has lots of twists, notably in the second half. Wolf Rilla also provided the careful and subtle direction and helps to imbue this with an un-nerving atmosphere. Fine production values are another reason that this works so well. Geoffrey Faithfull's great photography, Ivan King's pleasing art direction and Ron Goodwin's eerie score all impress. A likeable and superior piece of science fiction.

CAST: George Sanders; Barbara Shelley; Michael Gwynne; Laurence Naismith; John Phillips; Richard Vernon; Thomas Heathcote; Martin Stephens; Peter Vaughan; Bernard Archard; Jenny Laird; Richard Warner; Charlotte Mitchell; John Stuart; Tom Bowman; Keith Pyott; Rosamund Greenwood; Alexander Archdale; Sheila Robins; Susan Richards. Many others.

PRODUCTION COMPANY–UK DISTRIBUTOR:

MGM British - MGM

AVAILABLE ON DVD

FILM STUDIO: MGM British Studios Borehamwood

LOCATIONS: Letchmore Heath, Hertfordshire and in and around Hertfordshire

CIRCUIT AND APPROXIMATE RELEASE DATE:

ABC - November 1960 - Cert A

RUNNING TIME ON TV: 73 minutes

FORMAT: Black and White

IN THE UK AROUND THE TIME OF RELEASE

NEWS: The novel Lady Chatterley's Lover by D H Lawrence was found not to be obscene after Penguin Books' sensational trial.

POP HITS: It's Now Or Never - Elvis Presley; Only The Lonely - Roy Orbison

POPULAR TV: Bootsie and Snudge (sitcom, ITV); Sunday Night at The London Palladium (variety series, ITV)

POPULAR NEW CARS: Austin A40 (Farina) (1958–1967); Ford Consul (MkII) (1956–1962)

THE WINSLOW BOY (1948)

RATING: **

SYNOPSIS: In September 1912, a newly retired bank official continues to live in Wimbledon with his family. His youngest son becomes a cadet at a naval college, but is expelled for stealing a postal order. Convinced of his innocence, his father employs a famous barrister to defend him.

REVIEW: A solid British drama, aimed squarely at a discriminating middle class audience It's a little dry and stuffy, but that's part of its rich Edwardian atmosphere, yet it's very "1948" too. The Terence Rattigan and Anatole De Grunwald script was adapted from Rattigan's 1946 stage play. It's acutely observed and highly intelligent and also full of warmth and humanity. A dozen or so scenes are deeply moving, notably Robert Donat's interrogation of the title figure. Donat turns in an excellent, wistful performance and everyone else is in top form too, notably Sir Cedric Hardwicke and Basil Radford (who appeared "By Permission of J Arthur Rank Organisation"). As for the direction, Anthony Asquith, an over-rated figure, handles this with great care and understanding. Andre Andrejew's highly atmospheric art direction and the fine photography of Frederick Young and O (Osmond) Borradaile (exteriors) are an integral part of the film's appeal. Also impressive is William Alwyn's fine score. A well rounded, sincere and touching film.

CAST: Robert Donat; Sir Cedric Hardwicke; Margaret Leighton; Basil Radford; Marie Lohr; Frank Lawton; Kathleen Harrison; Neil North; Francis L Sullivan; Jack Watling; Stanley Holloway; Cyril Ritchard; Walter Fitzgerald; Ernest Thesiger; Mona Washbourne; Kynaston Reeves; Edward Lexy; Nicholas Hannen; Hugh Dempster; W A Kelly; Gordon McLeod; Ivan Sampson; Marie Michelle; Charles Groves; Vera Cook; Evelyn Roberts. UNBILLED CAST: Colin Gordon; David Horne.

PRODUCTION COMPANY–ORIGINAL UK DISTRIBUTOR:

London Films - Anatole De Grunwald/British Lion

AVAILABLE ON DVD

FILM STUDIO: London Film Studios, Shepperton

CIRCUIT AND APPROXIMATE RELEASE DATE:

ABC – November 1948 – Cert U

RUNNING TIME ON TV: 113 minutes

FORMAT: Black and White

NOTE: This was based on a real case from 1910.The cadet was George Archer-Shee, who later died at the first battle of Cyprus in 1914 aged 19. Coincidentally the director here was the son of the 1912 Liberal Prime Minister Herbert Asquith who is mentioned by Stanley Holloway.

IN THE UK AROUND THE TIME OF RELEASE

NEWS: Prince Charles is born to Princess Elizabeth.

POPULAR NEW CARS: Morris Six (1948–1953); Hillman Minx (Phase III) (1948–1949)

THE WITCHES (1966)

RATING: *

SYNOPSIS: After a horrifying witchcraft incident in Africa, a middle aged teacher accepts a teaching post in a village's private school, following an interview with someone who she assumes is a vicar. Are the strange incidents that subsequently take place linked to local witchcraft activity?

REVIEW: A ragged, but enjoyable Hammer horror at its best in the first hour, after which it gets a bit shaky and silly. Nigel Kneale's script, based on a novel "The Devil's Own" is an odd blend of the subtle and the simple minded. It depicts village life which is comfortable on the surface and chilling underneath. The direction from Cyril Frankel is efficient and he handles the lovely Hambleden, Buckinghamshire locations with style. Basically a daft cartoon strip, but it does possess a peculiar charm. Good, eerie score by Richard Rodney Bennett. Warning: extremely dumb in the last fifteen minutes.

CAST: Joan Fontaine; Kay Walsh; Alec McCowen; Gwen Ffrangcon–Davies; John Collin; Ingrid Brett; Leonard Rossiter; Michele Dotrice; Carmel McSharry; Martin Stephens; Ann Bell; Bryan Marshall; Shelagh Fraser; Viola Keats. UNBILLED CAST: John Barrett.

PRODUCTION COMPANY–ORIGINAL UK DISTRIBUTOR:

Hammer Film Productions – Warner-Pathe Distributors

AVAILABLE ON DVD

FILM STUDIO: Bray

LOCATIONS: Hambleden, Buckinghamshire

CIRCUIT AND APPROXIMATE RELEASE DATE:

ABC - December - 1966 - Cert X Supported by "Death Is A Woman" (GB "B" film Cert X)

RUNNING TIME ON TV: 87 minutes

FORMAT: Technicolor

IN THE UK AROUND THE TIME OF RELEASE

NEWS: Harry Roberts, John Whitney and John Duddy were sentenced to life imprisonment for the fatal shooting of three policemen.

POP HITS: Green Green Grass Of Home – Tom Jones; Good Vibrations –The Beach Boys

POPULAR TV: Coronation Street (ITV); Double Your Money (quiz show, ITV)

POPULAR NEW CARS: Humber Sceptre (1961–1967); Fiat 124 (1966–1974)

WITCHFINDER GENERAL (1968)

RATING: *

SYNOPSIS: In 1645, during the English Civil War, a cruel and obsessed lawyer, Matthew Hopkins and his assistant travel throughout Oliver Cromwell's stronghold of East Anglia. He's employed to interrogate and hang anyone suspected of witchcraft. His latest victim is a priest whose niece is the lover of one of Cromwell's roundhead soldiers. She pleads for his life and sleeps with Hopkins, but her uncle, after being tortured is hanged anyway. Both she and her lover determine to track down Hopkins to get revenge.

REVIEW: An above average "exploitation" picture, a hard edged, uncompromising and stylish affair. The director here, Michael Reeves died aged 25, soon after the film's release, from accidental barbiturate poisoning, following a spell of depression. He had enormous potential and it's interesting to speculate what he might have achieved had he lived. Judging by this he had a tremendous future. Here he displays real flair and a passion for landscape, rare in the British cinema, the location sequences here being extensive and beguiling. The script by Tom Baker (not the former Dr Who) and Michael Reeves, with additional scenes by M. Heyward is somewhat cobbled together. Things are helped by John Coquillon's fine Eastmancolor photography and the lovely score by Paul Ferris. As for Vincent Price (Reeves wanted Donald Pleasence), this is probably his best ever screen performance - he was told not to ham it up and is chilling and brilliant.

CAST: Ian Ogilvy; Hilary Dwyer; Nicky Henson; Rupert Davies; Patrick Wymark; Robert Russell; Wilfred Brambell; Godfrey James; Tony Selby; Margaret Nolan; Peter Haigh; Bernard Kay; Hira Talfrey; Sally Douglas. Also others.

PRODUCTION COMPANY–ORIGINAL UK DISTRIBUTOR:

Tigon British/American International – Tigon

AVAILABLE ON DVD

FILM STUDIO: None

LOCATIONS: Lavenham, Orford Castle, Kentwell Hall and others in Suffolk

CIRCUIT AND APPROXIMATE RELEASE DATE:

ABC – May 1968 - Cert X - Double bill supported by "The Blood Beast Terror"

RUNNING TIME ON TV: 81 minutes

FORMAT: Eastmancolor

IN THE UK AROUND THE TIME OF RELEASE

NEWS: Ronnie Kray and Reggie Kray are arrested for murder, blackmail and other crimes.

POP HITS: What A Wonderful World and Cabaret – Louis Armstrong; Lazy Sunday – The Small Faces

POPULAR TV: Coronation Street (ITV); Opportunity Knocks (talent show, ITV)

POPULAR NEW CARS: Ford Cortina 1600E (1967–1970); Hillman Hunter (1966–1977)

THE OTHER ONE STAR FILMS

I have only chosen 100 films for this book which includes the best of the one star films. Unfortunately there is not enough space to include the following one star films that I have also reviewed:

The Admirable Crichton (1957)
The African Queen (1951)
Alfie (1966)
The Amorous Prawn (1962)
And Now For Something Completely Different (1971)
Angels One Five (1952)
The Angry Silence (1960)
The Astonished Heart (1950)
Bachelor Of Hearts (1958)
Beau Brummell (1954)
The Bedford Incident (1965)
Beyond This Place (1959)
Billy Liar (1963)
The Birthday Party (1970)
Black Narcissus (1947)
Blanche Fury (1948)
Blind Terror (1971)
The Blue Lamp (1950)
The Blue Peter (1955)
Born Free (1965)
The Boys (1962)
The Bridal Path (1959)
The Bridge On The River Kwai (1957)
Brief Encounter (1945)
Brighton Rock (1947)

Burnt Evidence ("B") (1954)
A Canterbury Tale (1944)
Captain Boycott (1947)
Captain Clegg (1962)
The Captive Heart (1946)
Carry On Again Doctor (1969)
Carry On Camping (1969)
Carry On Cruising (1962)
Carry On Matron (1972)
Carry On Screaming (1966)
Carve Her Name With Pride (1958)
Cast A Dark Shadow (1955)
The Challenge (1960)
The Charge Of The Light Brigade (1968)
Charley Moon (1956)
Checkpoint (1956)
Chitty Chitty Bang Bang (1968)
The Clouded Yellow (1950)
The Comedy Man (1963)
Crooks Anonymous (1962)
Daleks Invasion Earth 2150 AD (1966)
Dangerous Cargo ("B") (1954)
A Day In The Death Of Joe Egg (1971)
The Day Of The Jackal (1973)
Deadly Nightshade ("B") (1953)
Dentist On The Job (1960)
Derby Day (1952)
Diamonds Are Forever (1971)
Don't Lose Your Head (1966) re-titled "Carry On, Don't Lose Your Head"
Double Bunk (1961)
Double Confession (1950)
Dr No (1962)
Dracula Prince Of Darkness (1965)

The End Of The Affair (1955)
The Entertainer (1960)
Entertaining Mr Sloane (1970)
Esther Waters (1948)
Fame Is The Spur (1947)
The Family Way (1966)
Fanatic (1965)
Fanny By Gaslight (1944)
Far From The Madding Crowd (1967)
Father Brown (1954)
Father Dear Father (1972)
Fire Down Below (1957)
First Men In The Moon (1964)
Footsteps In The Fog (1955)
The Franchise Affair (1951)
Frenzy (1972)
The Gentle Trap ("B") (1960)
Get Carter (1970)
Goldfinger (1964)
Gone To Earth (1950)
The Good Companions (1957)
Good Time Girl (1948)
The Gorgon (1964)
The Greengage Summer (1961)
The Guinea Pig (1948)
The Guns Of Navarone (1961)
The Hasty Heart (1949)
The Haunting (1963)
Heaven Knows Mr Allison (1957)
Hell Is A City (1959)
The Hellfire Club (1961)
Help! (1965)
Here We Go Round The Mulberry Bush (1967)

The Hi-Jackers ("B") (1963)
The Hill (1965)
HMS Defiant (1962)
Hobson's Choice (1954)
Horror Of Dracula (1958)
The Hound Of The Baskervilles (1959)
The Huggetts Abroad (1949)
Hunted (1952)
I See A Dark Stranger (1946)
I Thank A Fool (1962)
Ice Cold In Alex (1958)
If... (1968)
The Importance Of Being Earnest (1952)
The Inn Of The Sixth Happiness (1958)
The Interrupted Journey (1949)
The Intruder (1953)
The Ipcress File (1965)
The Iron Maiden (1962)
Island Of Terror (1966)
The Italian Job (1969)
Johnny Nobody (1961)
The Jokers (1966)
Josephine And Men (1955)
The Key (1958)
A Kid For Two Farthings (1955)
Kidnapped (1960)
The Kidnappers (1953)
King And Country (1964)
The L- Shaped Room (1962)
The League Of Gentlemen (1960)
The Leather Boys (1963)
Life At The Top (1965)
Live Now Pay Later (1962)
The Loneliness Of The Long Distance Runner (1962)

The Long Ships (1964)
Lost (1956)
Love Story (1944)
Lucky Jim (1957)
Lust For Life (1956)
Made In Heaven (1952)
Man On The Run (1949)
The Man Upstairs (1958)
The Man Who Never Was (1956)
The Masque Of The Red Death (1964)
A Matter Of Life And Death (1946)
The Mercenaries (1968)
The Mind Benders (1962)
The Mouse On The Moon (1963)
Mr Denning Drives North (1951)
Mr Perrin And Mr Traill (1948)
Murder At The Gallop (1963)
My Brother's Keeper (1948)
The Net (1953)
Never Let Go (1960)
The Night of The Demon (1957)
Night Of The Eagle (1962)
A Night To Remember (1958)
Nightmare (1964)
Obsession (1949)
Oliver Twist (1948)
One Way Out ("B") (1955)
Our Mother's House (1967)
Passage Home (1955)
A Place To Go (1963)
Please Turn Over (1959)
Pool Of London (1951)
Private's Progress (1956)
A Prize Of Arms (1962)

The Pumpkin Eater (1964)
The Punch And Judy Man (1962)
The Pure Hell Of St Trinian's (1960)
Reach For The Sky (1956)
The Red Beret (1953)
Ring Of Spies (1963)
Run Wild, Run Free (1969)
The Running Man (1963)
Ryan's Daughter (1970)
Sapphire (1959)
Scott Of The Antarctic (1948)
Scrooge (1951)
Scrooge (1970)
Seven Days To Noon (1950)
The Shiralee (1957)
Sink The Bismarck! (1960)
The Small Back Room (1949)
So Long At The Fair (1950)
Sons And Lovers (1960)
The Spanish Gardener (1956)
Spring In Park Lane (1948)
The Square Ring (1953)
A Stitch In Time (1963)
Stolen Hours (1963)
A Study In Terror (1965)
Summer Holiday (1963)
Sunday Bloody Sunday (1971)
Swiss Family Robinson (1960)
Take My Life (1947)
Tales From The Crypt (1972)
Tamahine (1963)
10 Rillington Place (1970)
Theater Of Blood (1973)
There's A Girl In My Soup (1970)

They Were Sisters (1945)
The Third Secret (1964)
This Is My Street (1963)
Those Magnificent Men In Their Flying Machines (1965)
The Three Lives Of Thomasina (1964)
Time Gentlemen Please! (1952)
Tom Brown's Schooldays (1951)
Too Many Crooks (1959)
The Trials Of Trials Of Oscar Wilde (1960)
Trio (1950)
The Triple Echo (1972)
Tunes Of Glory (1960)
Twisted Nerve (1968)
Two For The Road (1967)
The Vault Of Horror (1973)
Very Important Person (1961)
The Virgin and The Gypsy (1970)
What A Carve Up! (1961)
When Eight Bells Toll (1971)
When The Bough Breaks (1947)
Where There's a Will ("B") (1955)
Whistle Down The Wind (1961)
Woman Of Straw (1964)
The Wrong Arm Of The Law (1962)
Yield To The Night (1956)
The Young Ones (1961)
Zulu (1963)

ABOUT THE AUTHOR

Andy Coleby has been reviewing films for a potential book for a long time. In the past he has been cinema reviewer for The Henley Standard. He also has reviews on the "Britmovie" website including "My Brother Jonathan", "Street Corner" and "When The Bough Breaks". He has personally written 1,500 reviews on British films made from 1944–1973 and has written 8,000 British and Hollywood film reviews.

Over the years he has met (very briefly) Dirk Bogarde, David Warner, Mel Smith, Jenny Agutter, Dave Allen and many more stars and has managed to be star struck and nearly dumbstruck when he did.

When he was in a comedy duo, he appeared at a charity event to try to save the old Regal cinema at Henley - on - Thames. However, he didn't have the nerve to approach fellow performers Robert Morley and Dinah Sheridan, but did chat to Joe Brown. He also regularly noticed Diana Dors, who went to a pub in Sunningdale in the mid 1970's and again did not have the courage to speak to her.

In 1982 he attended the De Leon Drama Summer School in Richmond, Surrey supervised by the De Leon sisters and was told "I like you" by Beatrice De Leon after his performance in a cut down version of Thornton Wilder's play "The Skin Of Our Teeth". Beatrice De Leon with her husband used to run the "Q" theatre from the 1920's onwards and helped to discover Sean Connery, Trevor Howard, Vivien Leigh, James Mason, Michael Wilding, Vanessa Redgrave and Dirk Bogarde. The first plays of Terence Rattigan were performed at the "Q" theatre too.

He is proudest of the fact that he knew the late John Howard Davies, ex-head of Light Entertainment at the BBC and Thames

Television. His many credits include "Fawlty Towers", "Monty Python's Flying Circus" and "Steptoe and Son". He was warned never to mention that he played Oliver Twist in the 1948 film of that name. He found him incredibly generous, affable and helpful when he was trying to get the comedy duo off the ground.

He used to go to the cinema a lot, but does not like multiplexes, which he is surrounded by. When he does go to the cinema now, his favourite is the "Everyman" at Winchester.

ACKNOWLEDGEMENTS AND RECOMMENDED BOOKS, PUBLICATIONS AND WEBSITES

The British Film Catalogue 1895–1985 by Denis Gifford – David and Charles

The British B Film by Steve Chibnall and Brian McFarlane

The Encyclopedia of British Film by Brian McFarlane

ABC The First Name In Entertainment By Allen Eyles

Odeon Cinemas 2 by Allen Eyles

Gaumont British Cinemas by Allen Eyles

British Cinema Of The 1950's The Decline of Deference by Sue Harper and Vincent Porter

British Sound Films The Studio Years 1928–1959 by David Quinlan

Leonard Maltin's Classic Movie Guide

Quinlan's Character Stars by David Quinlan

The Guinness Top 40 Charts by Paul Gambaccini, Tim Rice and Jonathan Rice

Guinness British Hit Singles

Octane Classic Car Price Guide 2010–1945–1990 Edited by Keith Adams

40 Years Of British Television by Jane Harboard and Jeff Wright

Alastair Sim by Mark Simpson

From the Internet:

Wikipedia
The Worldwide Guide To Movie Locations
IMDB
news.bbc.co.uk/onthisday
Scotlandthemovie.com - Doug Hill

I would like to express my gratitude to Thelma who saw me through this book, provided support, offered comments, assisted in the editing, proofreading and design.

A special thanks to Pete Mowbray, author of “The Serpent Of The Valois” for his help and encouragement.

Lightning Source UK Ltd.
Milton Keynes UK
UKOW04f0618210917
309610UK00001B/116/P

9 781781 486580